Once Upon
An
Eskimo Time

Once Upon An Eskimo Time

EDNA WILDER

University of Alaska Press
Fairbanks

University of Alaska Press
P.O. Box 756240
Fairbanks, AK 99775-6240

ISBN 978-1-60223-056-9

Library of Congress Cataloging-in-Publication Data
Wilder, Edna, 1916–
Once upon an Eskimo time : a year of Eskimo life before the White man
  came as told to me by my wonderful mother whose Eskimo name was
  Nedercook / Edna Wilder.
p. cm.
Originally published: Edmonds, Wash. : Alaska Northwest Pub. Co.,
  c1987. ISBN 978-1-60223-056-9 (alk. paper)
1. Tucker, Minnie, ca. 1858–1979. 2. Wilder, Edna, 1916–
  —Family. 3. Eskimos—Alaska—Biography. 4. Eskimo women—
  Alaska—Biography. 5. Eskimos—Alaska—Social life and customs.
  6. Seward Peninsula (Alaska)—Biography. 7. Seward Peninsula
  (Alaska)—Social life and customs. I. Title.
E99.E7T838 2009
979.8004'971—dc22
[B]   2008051330

Cover design by Dixon Jones, UAF Rasmuson Library Graphics
Cover images: Geese and raven courtesy of U.S. Fish and Wildlife Ser-
vice, AK/RO/01386 and WO-Lee Karney-2838. Photo of Nedercook by
Mrs. Kenen. Photo of dancer and drummers by Lomen brothers; Alaska
State Library George A. Parks Collection, Photographs, 1911–1933,
ASL-PCA-240. Background: White Mountain, Anchorage Museum at
Rasmuson Center Library & Archives, AMRC-b83-82-4.

This publication was printed on acid-free paper that meets the minimum
requirements for ANSI / NISO Z39.48–1992 (R2002) (Permanence of
Paper for Printed Library Materials).

CONTENTS

FOREWORD

This book represents the first segment of the long-awaited saga on the life of "Grandma" Minnie Tucker, whose Eskimo name was Nedercook and whose life span probably covered 121 years from 1858 to 1979.

There were no written records in her Rocky Point village in those days, but certain events of the time indicate that Nedercook could have been 121 at the time of her death — and no one is around to dispute her birth date.

As remarkable as Nedercook is her daughter, Edna Tucker Wilder Cryan, who is an excellent artist, sculptor, photographer and writer. Her book on skin sewing is one of the most popular books published by Alaska Northwest Publishing Company.

I first met Edna a few years ago, when she signed up for a magazine-article writing course I was teaching at the University of Alaska. Like many of her fellow students in the class, Edna Wilder was a mature adult whose lifetime in Alaska gave her much material to write about. As usual, I asked each student for a list of ten ideas for magazine articles. When they came to their first weekly individual conferences, I would ask which one they wanted to write about first.

Edna Wilder did not hesitate.

"I'd like to start writing about my mother," she said.

"Well," I said, "everyone has a mother. What is there about *your* mother that others would want to read about?"

Edna may have been slightly taken aback, but she didn't show it.

"Well," she began, "I don't know, exactly, but she's lived all her life in Alaska and is about 110 years old."

My interest perked up. "A hundred and ten? And still alive? Is she able to communicate?"

"Oh, yes," said Edna. "She gets around pretty well and still sews, but has a bit of trouble reading her Bible. She's living alone in her own little cabin on Dawson Street. She bakes bread every day and chops kindling for her fire. She still walks to the store to buy her groceries except when she needs a lot of heavy things, like a large bag of flour, and I'll drive her to the store."

I was invited to take pictures in the little cabin of this remarkable lady, keeping the fire going and baking bread — and I can still remember the delicious smell and taste of that homemade bread baked by that gracious 110-year-old lady.

When it came time to photograph her walking to the store, she took a cane because it was very slick out. She didn't want to fall again and break another hip, as she had done at the tender age of 108 or 109. The doctors had told her quietly that she would never walk again.

Grandma Tucker could not accept this, of course, but was too embarrassed to use the walker in the hospital while others were watching. She waited until everyone else had gone to bed and then walked up and down the corridors alone, practicing until she was well enough to trade in the walker for a cane, then giving that up eventually.

This book, however, is not about Grandma as a magnificent old lady, but covers a year of her life as a young girl, just as Nedercook remembered it and as Edna Wilder took it down, including all the stories told by Nedercook's parents before the white man first came to their village on Norton Sound.

This book is a valuable contribution to the understanding of life on the tundra and an important segment of a remarkable life.

Jimmy Bedford
Professor of Journalism Emeritus
University of Alaska

INTRODUCTION

My mother, Nedercook, was a remarkable woman. She would have been that in any society at any time. This will be her story, as she told it to me while recovering from a broken hip during 1967-68, at the age of 109. Included will be stories and legends from her village, which she feared might be lost.

I took the notes originally so my two sons would know of the struggles their grandmother and her people endured uncomplainingly in a land that had no electricity, refrigerators, stores, matches, cars or any of civilization's other comforts. There were only the things of nature: space, tundra, sea, snow, land and sea animals, birds and the Eskimos of her village, Rocky Point, Alaska. Other villages were miles away and could be reached only by walking or paddling a skin boat or kayak on the generally turbulent Bering Sea during summer; in winter movement was by foot, or, occasionally, by a few men on village business using a community dog team.

I shall describe the primitive ways and means by which this hardy group of people lived and gathered and preserved their food. It may seem to the reader that they were always out to get or kill something — bird, fish, or animal. This was true back in the earlier days of Nedercook's life because there was no other way to survive in this harsh land, no other way for them to get food. They did not kill for sport, but rather for the food and clothing necessary for life itself.

I have concentrated on the year that Nedercook was about ten years old, probably about 1868. It was before the white man came to her village. She had an instinct and training for survival. Her happiness came from the small things of life and her own creativity with somewhat limited materials. Perhaps one of her most valuable talents was to see clearly, both physically and psychologically, later in life.

Nedercook did not see a white man until she was nearing her teens. Then the first was a sailor who had jumped ship or was put ashore by whalers or explorers. He had light brown hair. When he walked into the village late one fall, she was so afraid of him that she hid. He could not speak their language, but the villagers quickly understood by his gestures that he was hungry. They fed him and he stayed at the community dwelling, which they called the Big Dance House.

When winter was nearly over he headed west on foot, going up the coast. The Eskimos called him *Sammy-sis-ko* because he mentioned the word "San Francisco" so often. He would bring his hand to his chest and then point seaward and say "San Francisco." Years later Nedercook still remembered and sang the song composed by villagers in which "Sammy-sis-ko" was mentioned.

My father, Arthur Samuel Tucker, was a well educated Englishman, who entered the North by way of Chilkoot Pass during the gold stampede of 1898. He did not strike it rich in Dawson, Yukon Territory. Later he and others floated down the Yukon River on a raft they had made, landing at St. Michael. From there, he went to the gold fields at Nome, Alaska. Later he went to Bluff, where he mined with enough success to make a living.

He met Nedercook at her village when she and another woman were both bedridden. A doctor cousin of my father's had given him a couple of medical books when he was passing through Montana on his way north. He brought the two women canned tomatoes by the case, along with some little white pills which may have been aspirins or vitamins. He asked them each to eat one can of tomatoes a day and to take one little pill each day. Soon the women could sit up and move their arms and legs. By spring both were walking. After that Nedercook was never sick. On January 28, 1910, they were married. Together they reared two sons and one daughter, me. Another son died during his second year, and still another was drowned at age ten.

During the spring of 1942, Father died in their home at Bluff. A couple of years later Nedercook moved to Fairbanks. Both of her sons were in the service and she wanted to be near her daughter. She lived a remarkable life for many years. On what was believed to be her one hundred and thirteeth birthday, Alaska's Governor Jay Hammond sent her greetings and a citation. She may have been older, as the Eskimos had no calendars, nor did they have any way of recording birthdays.

This book is written to reveal a typical year of Nedercook's childhood. The stories and customs of the Eskimos included are strictly the ones belonging to the life style of the old village of Rocky Point. I have included only the stories, legends and beliefs which she told me. Those that are incomplete in this book are so because I do not have the whole story in Nedercook's words.

As the years passed, Nedercook became known in Fairbanks and by the press as the beloved "Grandma Tucker," but this story is of a young girl's early experiences.

Kiachook said that the hardest thing way back in the Eskimo history was once when there seemed like a double winter . . . a time with out the usual summer. This made very hard times that were difficult to live through.

ACKNOWLEDGMENTS

Writing a book requires help from a lot of people. I especially want to acknowledge and thank Jimmy Bedford, Professor of Journalism Emeritus, University of Alaska, Fairbanks, for writing the foreword to this book and for his help and encouragement. I also wish to acknowledge the inspiration, help, patience and understanding of my husband, Alexander P. Cryan. Others who have helped in a variety of ways that I won't detail here are: Harry C. Olson, Antonia R. Wilder, Nancy Lee Baker, Isabel M. Harper, Kay J. Kennedy and Jerome E. Lardy. Thank you one and all.

Edna Wilder

Description of an Inne

The inne had one doorway with steps so you could climb down into the shed. Off to one side of the shed was the stormy day cook room with heavy furs hung to close a doorway to keep the heat in. There was a skylight in the ceiling to let the smoke out.

A longer passageway led to the main living quarters. There were furs hung to close doorways and to keep the cold out. The main living quarters had a fireplace in the center with a skylight above. The walls and roof were of wood with straw behind the wood for insulation. The inne was an underground dwelling.

LIST OF CHARACTERS AND NAMES

Nedercook (Ned´-er-cook) . . . Girl in the story, later known as Grandma Tucker.

Inerluk (In´-er-luk) . . . her father

Kiachook (Ki´-ach-ook) . . . her mother

Nutchuk (Nut´-chuk) . . . her older brother

Paniagon (Pa´-nia-gon) . . . her older sister

Oolark (Oo´-lark) . . . her older brother, but younger than Nutchuk

Kimik (Kim´-ik) . . . Paniagon's husband

Komo (Ko´-mo) . . . Kimik's dog

Oopick (Oo´-pick) . . . oldest woman of the village

Inne (In´-ee) . . . underground house, with skylight.

Big Dance House . . . Large underground meeting house here ceremonies and meetings are held, and emergency supplies and live coals are kept. It has a side room for bath or steam bath. Unmarried men and visiting men sleep here.

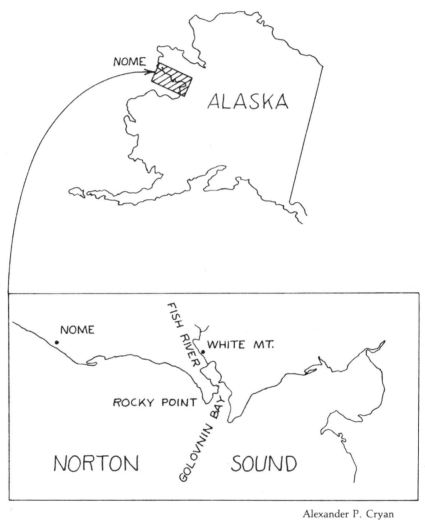

ALASKA

NOME

NOME

FISH RIVER

WHITE MT.

ROCKY POINT

GOLOVNIN BAY

NORTON   SOUND

Alexander P. Cryan

CHAPTER 1
FIRST GOOSE

S pring," Nedercook said softly as she lifted her face toward the sky. There was evident joy and relief in her whispered words. "It is spring." She breathed deeply of the sweet spring air, which caressed her face. The sun, which was already climbing the sky, touched her cheek and also brought out a sparkle on the distant waters of the Bering Sea. She walked toward the knoll above their inne. There she would be able to look over most of the village and along the beach to where the cliffs began in the west. For eons the small settlement had snuggled into the hillside of this rocky projection on the Seward Peninsula. The point of land extended into the Bering Sea for about 12 miles (Latitude 64°24′ North; Longitude 163°8′ West) and is marked on the map of Alaska only as Rocky Point.

Nedercook stood tall upon the knoll. She was looking and listening. On the far side of the village a dog barked. She could hear faintly the happy voices of children at play. A great feeling of joy filled her being — maybe it was knowing that the cold, dark days of winter had passed for another year.

Racing back to the inne, her home, she arrived just as her father was saying to her brothers, "Today we go on big hunt." The ice in front of the village had gone out, leaving only floating chunks drifting about.

She ran down to the beach where her mother and others were putting things in little piles in preparation for leaving. "You eat good," her mother said with a wave of her hand toward the inne. She raced back up the

1

incline and dashed down the few steps to the underground passageway. This led into the large circular room that was the main dwelling. She remembered that it was a good idea to eat, but she was so excited it was hard for her to get more than a couple of swallows down. She put some dry fish in her pack, with her meager personal things, picked up her bow and arrows, and carried them all to the beach.

Finally, with much waving to her friends who were left on the beach, the big oomiak (skin boat) left. It was followed by several men, each in his kayak. They headed west following the coastline. Sea birds of many kinds flew by, making many different sounds, while others swam and then flew as they approached. Others dived, only to appear and dive again.

As they traveled slowly westward they would continue to paddle and hunt until they reached a stretch of ice that still clung to the beach. Here they would camp, hunt, and dry meat for the winter until that section of ice floated away, and then they would go on to the next section of solid ice. If none was reached they would go as far as Ararchuk (Cape Nome), where they would camp for a while before returning home. On the third day they reached solid ice, so the oomiak came to shore just east of the ice on the beach, where camp was temporarily set up.

The next morning a very dense fog surrounded them. Geese and ducks flew very low as they followed the shoreline, making loud calls as they winged westward in great flocks. Nedercook felt excited as she listened to the sounds of numerous geese approaching, louder and louder, until the whole air seemed to vibrate with the sound. She would catch sight of them for a minute or two as they passed, only to be lost again. Mingled with the sounds of the eider ducks came the almost groaning, grunting, moaning sounds of the walrus. These strange sounds came to her from out in the fog.

2

There seemed to be so many, some close and some so far out that she could just hear them. The noises sounded to her as if they were moving west, but Nedercook knew that the ice angled out from their camp, because she had seen it the evening before the fog drifted in.

The hunters also heard the sounds and made preparations for a hunt. Before leaving camp her father, Inerluk, had instructed all the hunters to stay close to one another during the fog. The kayaks were manned and quietly disappeared into the fog. For just a short time Nedercook thought she could hear the dip of the paddles, then the sounds of the birds and animals took over.

She decided to fish for tomcod. Her mother warned her not to go out onto the ice or wander back on the tundra. She took her packsack, bow, arrows, and the fishing line. As she walked westward the camp disappeared behind her in the fog. She walked and walked, expecting any minute to reach the ice that angled seaward. She knew that she could not miss it because she was following the edge of the open water.

After a time she sat on a rock. Looking up, she saw some rocks jutting even higher, so she climbed up on these and sat down. The fog seemed even denser here. Then she heard another flock of geese call and from the sound she knew they were flying low. Their calls became louder and louder. Soon the whole air seemed to vibrate with the sound. They must be very low. Quickly she placed an arrow in her bow and pulled it taut. When she saw them they were almost in line with her and the rock. She stood up. The geese saw her and tried to turn, making a dense mingling of wings and bodies. She let her arrow fly into the thickest area. It missed the first two, but then one bird came down, hitting the ice on the edge of the fog. Quickly she scrambled down the rocks and began running toward it. She saw it flop and, as it did, it fell from the shore ice into the sea water. She ran faster but it was out of reach. It was still floating.

3

She tried throwing her fish hook, but it always fell short. Then she placed the fishing gear on the ice where it could be easily seen and headed for the beach. She found a long pole where the tides of last fall had left it. Carrying this, she ran back to the water's edge until she spotted the fishing gear and then the goose. She looked for a chunk of floating ice large enough to carry her weight. Reaching with the pole, she pulled it slowly closer until she could jump onto it. It did not move fast, but it did move, as she poled and paddled with the long stick. She

was so eager to get the goose that as she reached to pick it up she nearly fell into the water. Then she had it on her chunk of ice. When she straightened up, she thought that she was lost in the fog because she could not see the edge of the ice. She looked at the sky. It seemed a little brighter in one direction, so she pushed toward the darker side. Soon she saw the fishing gear near the edge of the ice.

She jumped off with her goose and pole the minute the ice cake touched the solid ice. She then stopped to examine her goose. It felt fat and heavy and she thought it looked beautiful. When she turned it in many directions, it still was beautiful. Reluctantly she put it into her packsack and swung it to her back. Picking up her fishing gear, bow and arrows, she started on. More flocks of geese flew by. For a while she would ready her arrow, but as the geese approached she could tell by the sound that they would be out of her arrow's reach. So she would put her arrow back into the pouch and walk on.

Suddenly she realized that, fog or no fog, she had walked too far without finding the ice she was looking for. Now she knew that it had floated away during the dense fog. The old-squaw ducks were making their calls from the water in front of her, but she could not see them. They sounded beautiful, so musical, she loved to listen to them. "Ar-ar-neak," she mimicked their calls for a while. The walrus sounds had moved so far to the west that she had to listen to hear them and then it was only an occasional faint sound. The fog was so dense that it was almost wet as she started back, following the shoreline. She traveled for a time and then stopped because she thought that she had heard her name called very faintly. Listening, she heard her mother's voice calling, "Daughter?"

"Mama!" she called back as she broke into a run along the uneven terrain in the direction of her mother's voice. Soon she could see her mother's figure. As she got closer she saw that her mother carried her walking stick. "Worried about you," her mother said, "You gone so long."

Nine-year-old Nedercook stood before her mother, tall for her age, her shiny black hair hung in a lone braid down her back, tied with a thin piece of skin. Mukluks covered her feet; skin pants and a light fur parka covered her body. Her dark eyes were shining with excitement. Wet fog fell on the soft brown skin of her face and hands.

She quickly removed her packsack and held it out to her mother. Kiachook took it as she sat down on a jutting rock. She knew from her daughter's expression that the pack held something special. Opening it slowly, she exclaimed "A-nic-ka," as her hand moved quickly to feel whether it was warm and fresh or a cold, dead found one. The goose was warm and there was fresh blood. Removing it her mother asked, "How?"

While Nedercook told her the excitement flowed through her again, but her mother did not seem pleased about her going out on the ice cake. Kiachook picked the goose there, as she believed the longer the feathers stayed on, the more fat they took off. Her daughter helped. Then for some time they sat quietly on the rocks, listening to the different sounds of spring.

"We go back," Kiachook finally said. "Maybe hunters come." Together they walked and Nedercook realized that she had gone much farther than she was aware of. As they approached the camp they could smell the smoke before it came into view. Nedercook remembered how they were instructed upon getting into the oomiak not to kick over the big pot, because it had a smaller pot inside with coals for the cooking fire. She also remembered the warm glow it radiated.

The hunters had not returned. Kiachook cut the goose in pieces and put it in one of the pots to cook. It was so foggy that it made the evening darker.

After what seemed a long time, they could hear the hunters returning long before they could see them. She knew that they were not hunting because they were too noisy. When they came into view she saw why they were so slow. They had rawhide leaders tied to a walrus they were towing. A cry went up from camp. As the kayaks came to shore the lines were taken by eager hands. Then everyone pulled on the lines and with much effort, both pulling and pushing, the animal was beached.

Eagerly they began cutting and skinning, while the

children built up the fire. Pots of meat were put on to cook. Others gathered poles from the beach, and a rough rack was soon standing. Pieces of meat were hung to dry and, because wood was plentiful, they had a nice community fire with someone from each family tending to that family's pot. Nedercook's goose that evening was only an appetizer, but it was delicious and praise was high.

That evening when they settled for the night, her father said, "Tell true story." He began;

This happened two years ago when there was a big famine. People at Cape Darby's village were starving because game was scarce and when game is scarce it always seems that everything edible is scarce — there is just nothing. During this time, in one inne two fellows of the village were still alive. One had a pot of some kind and at mealtimes he would heat water, sip and drink it, just as if he were having soup. The other fellow wore a squirrel parka and each day he would take a couple of bites from his skin parka. Each day they tried to hunt, but there was nothing. They did this day after day, fishing also, but nothing. One day in early spring the tomcod returned. They fished tomcod and survived the famine.

When her father finished he spoke again of the hard times they had had two years ago. As Nedercook lay on her meager bed she remembered the famine.

When it became evident there was a famine, each family brought all its food and put it in the stormy-day room. This was standard procedure because the less one's body was used, the less it demanded. All unnecessary trips to the cache were eliminated. Nedercook remembered very clearly the amount of food she ate each day. It was so small she was always hungry. It was down to a small bite of dry salmon or whale, but her mother kept the pots filled with warm water and when she complained of being hungry her mother told her to drink of the water. She remembered the days when there was nothing left to eat.

Lying in the semi-darkness, she relived the days of hunger. Many of the villagers had died by the time it was finally over. Hunters left every day, and returned with nothing. Three hunters had failed to return since the beginning of the famine; all three had hunted on different days and each failed to return. The villagers believed that the men in desperation had hunted too far and too long for what strength they had left, and had died before they could reach home. Others who had not hunted died in their innes.

During this time, although her mother did not say anything, Nedercook knew she was worried because their men were gone all day.

Nedercook recalled that, except for the small glowing coals, they had no light because when famine strikes the seal oil lamp is one of the first things to go. Oil becomes too valuable to burn in lamps when it could be used for food. After dark they sat listening . . . listening . . . listening. They knew they were not the only ones in the dark.

As long as Nedercook lived she would remember hearing the men arrive, and how great the joy to find a seal being lowered down the outer steps of the entrance way, followed by her father and brothers. She remembered her mother touching the seal in the dim light, running her hands over its body while she cried in happiness. She recalled the excitement as they dragged the seal into the big room! She had never seen a whole seal in this, the living and sleeping room, before, but this was different. This meant — life.

Her sister, Paniagon, started adding fuel to the fire, and set the pots of hot water nearer it. No one worried about saving the seal's skin, they cut it open in front. Paniagon scooped up the blood and juices and added them to the hot water, which cooked it quickly. Then they drank this thin blood soup. Everyone was too hungry to wait long. As soon as little pieces were cut off they were put on little sticks and roasted until barely warm, and eaten with pieces of blubber and more soup. Never in her life had anything tasted so good to Nedercook.

As her father and mother satisfied their appetites, they moved to their beds and fell asleep. Her brothers, who for years had slept at the Big Dance House, did not try to go there, but rather moved to their old beds. Without removing their garments, they lay down in a half circle and fell asleep. The two sisters stayed up, cooking with all the cooking pots they could arrange by the fire while they waited for it to die down for the night. Finally they gave up and Nedercook remembered only going toward her bed.

All happily ate from the pots of cooked food the next morning and Nedercook took a big pot of cooked soup, meat and blubber to Oopick (the oldest woman in the village). She was lying in her bed weak from hunger, but she sat up when she saw Nedercook coming toward her. Tears filled her old eyes. Crying in gratitude, she drank of the soup and ate some of the meat that Nedercook cut in small pieces.

Nedercook and her brothers made trips around the village carrying pieces of seal to the main families. They, in turn, would share their gifts with their relatives. Some of the lone poor came to Inerluk for any scrap they could get. They were not disappointed. All the seal was soon distributed. There was much rejoicing as everyone had some part of it.

Inerluk carried the seal's head down to the sea (His wife had given the seal a drink of fresh water the first evening). She always saved a little of the water to toss in the entrance way of their inne. The custom of giving the seal a drink of fresh water was carried out by all the villagers. They believed that it showed their thanks and insured them of more in the future. Then the seal's head was dropped back into the salty water. Tomcod returned a couple of days later and the whole village fished and grew stronger. Then they hunted.

We are so lucky this year, Nedercook thought as she drifted off to sleep.

CHAPTER 2

MIRACLE MAN

N ext morning the fog lifted and a breeze made for
perfect drying conditions. They decided to
remain camped where they were for a few days,
while the meat dried enough to be put into seal pokes
with some blubber, which would render itself to oil.

On the third morning everything was loaded into the
oomiak and they started for Cape Nome. This village
was known for its many miracle men and one woman
the people called, "The woman who heals with her
hands." It was said that by moving her hands over one's
body she would discover what was wrong. She could

when necessary open the body and remove the offending part, then close it to heal immediately.

Upon reaching Cape Nome they made camp on the beach, where they set up another crude drying rack and hung up any meat that was not dry enough.

Next day the men took the big oomiak and the kayaks out to hunt, as there were still many pieces of floating ice. Walrus and seals climbed on these to sun themselves. The hunters had been at sea a short time when a very, very strong wind from the north suddenly started to blow. From the shore, whitecaps blew out to sea. Everyone feared the hunters would never return.

The wind continued to blow for two days. When the hunters still did not return, the families were so worried that the people of Cape Nome decided to call a meeting. After all of the missing men's families had gathered at the Big Dance House, the spokesman for the Cape Nome villagers asked one of their miracle men whether he could "see" and tell them what had happened to the hunters.

The big room was crowded as everyone gathered there, including Nedercook. The miracle man asked for a bucket of water. Nedercook was all eyes as she watched a middle-aged man carry in a wooden bucket. Water came to within three inches of the top. It was placed on the floor near the center of the room. Then the miracle man slowly, very slowly began swaying his body slightly from side to side while he slowly circled around the bucket of water. He began to chant or sing, "I use this bucket as a dip net to find what I wish . . . Oh! let me too perceive or see what has happened to these people." He repeated this over and over as he slowly circled the bucket of water. His eyes gazed steadily into the water. Never did his eyes leave the water, nor did they lose the intense look as he slowly continued to circle.

Nedercook was fascinated by this miracle man and his movements, so to her it seemed like a very short time until he abruptly stopped and exclaimed, "Oh! I see that they have landed safely down the coast between Solomon and Spruce Creek." The people were relieved and joyful.

A few days later the wind stopped. On the second day afterward the hunters came paddling back. Sure enough, they had been forced to beach and had stayed at the very place the miracle man had "seen" in the bucket of water.

Everyone was happy to see the hunters return. Nedercook especially was happy to see her father and brothers because she, too, had feared they might be dead.

Usually the hunters hunted until the ice moved too far away, but now that the big north wind had taken the ice away for good, the Inerluk family decided to return to their village. The weather was warmer going back and seal hunting was fairly good, so they decided to take some home whole and prepare them at the village.

They had planned to stop at Cliff Village on the way back so Kiachook could get some clay for pots and plates, but the big oomiak was filled with partly dried meat and many pokes of blubber. Instead they decided to make a trip for clay later in the summer, if possible. If they continued home now there still would be a little time left for squirrel hunting.

After reaching the village and unloading the boat everyone was tired. Each was happy to get back to his own bed, even though it was only a woven grass mat with a caribou skin on it for a mattress. As she was falling asleep Nedercook thought how nice and soft her bed was.

CHAPTER 3

SQUIRREL HUNTING

The next couple of days were busy, hurried days and there was no time for storytelling. The kill from the trip was distributed among the crew and they in turn gave of their share to the village people. If only one walrus was taken, it was customarily kept by the owner of the oomiak; he, in turn, could either keep it or give it away. Walrus skin, being heavy and thick, had to be split, a tiresome, hard job with primitive tools, but if this was done the skin would separate and become the equivalent of two hides. This skin could be used to cover an oomiak, or to make soles for mukluks, or rawhide which was used for laces, nets and ropes. The men would remove the ivory tusks later. Now they were helping to care for the meat and skins. Some of the sealskin was used for oil pokes (containers) and some was stretched and dried for clothing. The oogruk's intestines were scraped so the membrane would be suitable for rain wear and for skylight coverings. The stomach was prepared and used for containers, and the windpipe, for leather. Each hunter preserved the bladder from his seal for display later at the Big Winter Festival. All this they did within two days, so the meat would not spoil. Those who could not help with the animals helped by cooking and preparing the meals.

Nedercook was still excited from the trip and from being home again. She was standing and eating meat from a bone. Kiachook noticed this and reminded her to sit down. "Make big thick legs if you always eat standing up," her mother said, as she had at other times in Nedercook's life when she forgot to sit down.

By the third day all the rush was finally over and the family gathered outdoors for the evening meal. All that was needed now was someone to turn the drying meat over on the racks every now and then, or cover it if it rained. What could not be covered was carried inside until the weather was better.

Inerlook did not want to go squirrel hunting this spring. He would stay and care for the meat, and set out the herring net, which also caught tomcod and trout. The two brothers wanted to continue seal hunting, as it would soon be time to go on the "big black whale hunt." They did not want to miss this, the greatest thrill of the season.

Some of the large male ground squirrels had been out of hibernation for about a week. Kiachook decided if they were to get any this spring the women should go out for them. Paniagon wanted some squirrel skins for a parka for Kimik, her husband. She had used all she had on the fancy parka she had made for herself before the big festival last year.

Kimik owned one of the few dogs of the village, a well-behaved dog, attached to both Kimik and his wife. "We take Komo." Paniagon said as they prepared for the trip. Kimik had used Komo for two years as a helper when he went hunting, and had made him a pack from skin. They filled Komo's pack with snares and some dry fish. Each of the women carried ulus (the ulu is an Eskimo woman's knife), rawhide (Eskimo rope and string), food, and a little pouch for the leg bones of the squirrels, which in those days were prized for needles. In addition, each carried some seal oil and one small wooden dish. The dish was used to hold the oil when eating dry fish, which they dipped in oil.

Nedercook took her bow and arrows. They would have to travel quite a distance on foot to reach the place of the gray limestone hills. There the adult male squirrels took on the gray color of the surrounding hills, the color most prized by the people of the village.

Komo was a good dog. He did not run away or leave Paniagon. He also did not chase the brown-necked ptarmigan that ran strutting around on the tundra as the women trudged along, nor did he chase the red foxes that occasionally barked from rocks on the hillsides.

They had traveled by night most of the time, as was customary at this time of the year. The snow became too soft in the daytime, and one would just waste time and energy wallowing in it, or walking farther to go around the patches of snow. At night it was frozen so they could all walk on the snow crust and have no fear of sinking in. It was still very cold at night so, even with their warm parkas, sleeping without any bedding was uncomfortable.

Finally they reached the base of the hills. This year Kiachook wanted to camp down by the dense willow growth, at the head of a little draw that came down from the hills. The sun was one quarter across the sky by the time they reached their camping spot. They were all tired

17

and Kiachook decided they should eat first, then make the camp. They removed their packs and when they removed Komo's he jumped around wagging his tail, happy to have the load off. The women turned their backs on one another as they ate. It was an old custom. If two or more women were out together, they could keep watch and the dreaded black bear could not sneak up unseen. This way they all ate in peace.

As they ate the warm sun beat down upon them, melting the snow and making little streams here and there. Nedercook listened to the Lapland longspur and watched as it flew up into the sky, to sing as it came gliding down again. She thought the colorful little bird was so pretty. Overhead a flock of geese was winging north. It was so peaceful and beautiful. There was a little spring pond in the grass below them on the open tundra and, while Nedercook was taking in this beautiful scene, a flock of whimbrels, curlew-like birds, decided to stop there to rest and refresh themselves. Their call was light, happy and clear; soon it was joined by the call of the pretty golden plover. The combination stirred an emotion in Nedercook as her dark eyes took in the snow patches on the bare ground, and the ever-changing color of the Bering Sea that stretched to the distant horizon and, above this, the clear blue sky of spring in Alaska. I wish I could keep this always in my mind, she was thinking, when her mother called, "Help make camp."

They walked from the bare knoll where they had been sitting, and waded into the soft snow under the willows. Finding a natural little clearing, they began tramping down the soft snow. Their mother gathered grass. Komo was chewing on some dead grass a little distance away. They put some willow shoots and twigs on the farthest side of the opening so they could lie down without being on the snow. Then they went to help their mother gather dead grass. It was scarce, but they took what they had and put it on their willow floor.

"We look now," Kiachook said. They looked up toward the hills, and saw little black spots on the white drifts that still remained on the hillsides. The spots were the gray male ground squirrels, which had tunneled through the snow and were sitting by their entrances. From a distance a squirrel looked black. The animal would sit by his entrance and sun himself for a little while each day, becoming accustomed to the light. As the days passed he would move farther and farther away from the hole and in a week or two, when the females and yearlings in the lower grounds came out of hibernation, he would run down to be with them. That is when the Eskimos usually gave up hunting squirrels, because the skins would become torn from fighting and the flesh, tough and tasteless. "You remember where you see them," their mother said as she continued, "We rest now." The women removed their mukluks and hung them to dry and air on the willows.

Nedercook awoke to her mother's voice, "We hunt close today." The sun had set and the black spots were gone. The women left everything in camp but the snares and some willow sticks. They started for the foothills, the mother taking the center, a daughter on either side. The snow on the tundra was not always predictable, some was hard and some, soft. The deeply drifted places where the snares were set were harder, so traveling was easier there. After setting snares they returned to camp.

"Tomorrow we make fire," Kiachook said, so mother and daughters spent the coldest part of the night scrounging for wood, which was small and scarce. As they gathered wood they piled it on the dry knoll. Komo wandered with them. Kiachook then showed her daughters where she wanted rocks and dirt removed for next day's fire. Using sticks, they dug all the loose unfrozen dirt away and pulled the rocks away until Kiachook was satisfied.

By then it was morning. Kiachook thought that they

19

should go farther around the hill while the snow was still hard. They would have something to eat there while looking for black spots, set their snares, and nap on the hill by the big rocks before heading back to camp.

Nedercook needed to relieve herself, so she went off and found a large rock, turned it over, and did her business where it had rested. She used a combination of leaves, grass and moss for wiping, threw this on top and turned the rock back. All children were taught to do this. If there was no rock, they dug a hole or found a crack in the tundra and covered the mess before going on.

They took more snares, food, sticks, and Komo. They would leave the camp unguarded. There was no need to be quiet so they talked as they walked. Ptarmigan were all over, plentiful and tame. They decided to get some for dinner. They had not brought a clay pot because of weight, but the ptarmigan needed only picking and warming by the fire before eating. They were not like the squirrel, which was cannibalistic and needed to be well cooked. They all used rocks to kill the ptarmigan. Years of practice had made their aim quite accurate and before long they had enough. Feeling hungry, they stopped to eat of the dry food. They had climbed some during the hunt and Nedercook was beginning to feel tired. Her sister fed Komo.

Many little black spots had appeared and again Kiachook warned her daughters not to go too far from each other and to keep a sharp lookout for the dreaded bear, as he, like the squirrels, would be awake from winter hibernation. With their mother taking the center again, they started off setting more snares.

They walked to the big rocks on the hill. It was like a little cliff with some larger boulders lying in front. Kiachook chose a nice, dry, sunny exposure where Komo would be able to rest in front while they napped. Kiachook plugged Nedercook's ears with some of the wild cotton she carried. She said it was to keep the many-legged insect that came out in the spring from entering her ears while she slept. The belief was that if one did, it would eat her brain and then come out of the other ear. Nedercook fell asleep as soon as she lay on the rough ground. She thought that she had just fallen asleep when someone was shaking her. Glancing in the direction of the sun, she knew she had slept for some time. Her mother had cleaned the ptarmigan and she had dug some of the wild Eskimo potatoes *(Hedysarum alpinum)*. Up this high, the ground thawed quickly after the snow left. The vegetable was firm and sweet at this time of year and it would remain so until the plant started to grow. It would not be picked after that until late fall, after the tops were dead and dry.

Kiachook told her daughters to check their snares. She would check hers. They were all lucky. They took the snares with them as they went because these were the holes of the large gray male squirrels, who lived alone. Later, when the females and yearlings came out, they could set the snares on the runways between holes, but not for long, because when the rutting season started the males would fight, tearing holes in the skins, and the meat became tasteless.

Going back Nedercook felt thirsty so she used a few fingers and dipped up the clean, water-laden snow. When they reached camp it felt like they were coming home. The three began skinning their catch. Hanging the skins to dry was easy, as they were by the willows. They hung the skins through the natural eye hole on a prong and soon the willows looked as if they were bearing long, dark fruit. The sun had long set by the time they had finished, but being spring, the nights did not get dark.

Kiachook and her daughters placed some green wood, damp grass, moss and leaves in the bottom of the fire hole. Kiachook then placed the squirrel meat on this to cook, leaving the heads and feet attached but first taking off the prized leg bones for needles. She placed the squirrels in the hole with the backs turned up, packing them in tightly. Then she put more damp grass and leaves on top. She placed some green willow sticks over this. She took her flints and some of the dry cotton she carried in a special bag made from the oogruk wind-pipe. She also carried a piece of birch bark. She assembled all this, tore the bark into small pieces, and broke little dry sticks. Then she began trying to make a spark. It took some time, but finally she had one. It caught in the cotton. Kiachook quickly nourished it into a flame. Once it started, she just added more bark and twigs. When the fire was safely burning and there was no danger of its going out, her daughters took over.

The fire felt good. "We eat ptarmigan." Kiachook said. They broke off long willow shoots to use as sticks to roast the ptarmigan. As the meat lost its bloody red color they tore off pieces and dipped them in seal oil. The hot food tasted good. Paniagon cooked the last two birds, while Nedercook gathered wood with Komo following her. As they did this the sun rose.

"We go over there," her mother said, gesturing toward the hills to the right. Nedercook was not eager to leaving the fire. They placed quite a bit of the slower-burning green wood over the fire hole. Paniagon instructed Komo to remain in camp.

The tussocks were frosted on the tundra and the damp places were slippery with ice, but as soon as the sun rose they would turn to water quickly. Leaving the rough ground behind, they climbed the hillside and, although it was sloping, it was easier walking. The trained eye could now find holes without the animals sitting in front. Finally their mother called a halt. The snow was getting too soft for easy walking. On the way back there were so many ptarmigan that they tried for some more. As they walked into camp Komo came to meet them wagging his tail and jumping for joy. The fire was still glowing so they added more fuel, cleaned the birds, removed their mukluks and lay down. Nedercook enjoyed the nice fresh potato roots with their meal. It was the first time she felt rested since coming on the trip.

Then they continued around the hill, picking up yesterday's snares, and were surprised to meet some people from their village. They sat and visited. Everyone was having good luck. They all decided to return to their individual camps because a wind had sprung up and a storm seemed on its way. Komo jumped with happiness as they came into camp.

"We eat," Kiachook said, pushing the coals out of the hole and to the side. She removed the well-cooked squirrels. They tasted delicious. Heads, feet and bones were given to Komo, who wagged his tail as he ate.

Quickly they strung and tied the dry skins in bundles of 40. This was the standard number used for a man's parka. They put the bundles in their packs because it looked like it was going to snow. When it snowed this late in the spring it was usually a messy, wet snowfall. Hurriedly they refilled the fire hole, packed meat as they had before, scraped all the coals back, and added more wood. The storm lasted one day and night. It was very unpleasant, especially since they had no shelter. They stayed in camp and kept the fire going by continually gathering wood.

CHAPTER 4
BEAR

Their days as they hunted were filled with wind, snow, rain and intense sunshine. Their faces and hands suffered most because of constant exposure to the elements. The bundles of 40 skins were now 2 and they had 20 skins hanging to dry, along with a lot of meat. "We get one more bundle, go home," their mother said.

Today they would cross over the lower section of the foothills, a low saddle between the hills. Foxes were seen every now and then, also many of the large northern or tundra hares. They did not try to get the hares because their mother was against killing any animal that was carrying young. They would wait until the berries were ripe; that was the time at which her village figured that any young was old enough to go without its parent, if the parent should be killed.

Over the hill the women branched out to hunt on the back slope. From there they could see for many miles. Nedercook looked far to the north and saw the dark lines that were the big spruce trees that she had heard of. Someday she hoped to go where the big trees grew, just to see what the trees were like. The very few trees she had seen she could count on her hands; they had tried to grow on the windswept tundra, managed to get only a couple of feet tall, and were spread along the ground as they struggled to survive against the strong winds.

Nedercook took off to the left as they started to set snares again. She had not gone far when she saw some large, large tracks in the snow! She had never seen tracks

24

like these before and she tried to imagine what it could be. She thought of waiting until snaring was over to tell her mother but then she decided to run and ask her mother what made these tracks. When Nedercook told her, Kiachook looked a moment in the direction she had been going, almost shrugged, and turned to follow her daughter.

Kiachook stood as if frozen, looking at the tracks. Nedercook, who was looking too, glanced at her mother's face and knew right away that her mother was scared. She could see it on her face.

"Uk-thluk," (bear) her mother almost stammered. Then she raised her eyes and scanned the hillsides, saying, "We go back."

Nedercook felt a kind of fearful panic seize her. She ran quickly to Paniagon, who was just about to set a snare. Nedercook's throat felt dry as she said in a hoarse whisper, "Bear come, we go." Her sister pulled up the

snare as they rushed to meet their mother. Her frightened eyes seemed to be looking everywhere.

"Take up snares," their mother said as they started back. Nedercook was scared as she left to gather her snares. The fear of the bear was contagious. Snares were hurriedly snatched up along with any squirrels caught. The snow was soft as they went back but they all seemed to have extra strength. Reaching camp and seeing Komo there, wagging his tail, was so very reassuring that the two sisters reached down and hugged him.

"We go home," Kiachook said in almost a whisper, trying to hide the fear she felt. They packed in a hurry, no one saying a word, filling the packs with skins and meat. The sun had set by the time they were ready to leave and the snow patches were starting to freeze for the night. There was no time even to eat.

As she walked, carrying her load, Nedercook looked in every direction. She had never seen a bear, but she knew it was to be feared because her mother feared it. This bear, she thought, must have phenomenal speed and strength, but she was too frightened to ask. The bear might have tremendous hearing power too. As they walked in silence she expected to see at any moment a furious creature come tearing over the ridge and like lightening come galloping over the tundra to devour them. She saw her mother and sister looking about as they hurried on.

As Nedercook struggled along in silence, she recalled the often repeated story of a man her parents knew as Chow-nie-go.

> One day while Chow-nie-go was out hunting in or along the edge of thick alder brush, he was suddenly attacked by a bear. Even before he could bring his spear into position the bear was biting him. (Chow-nie-go was known as a very strong man, tough and a good hunter.) He pulled out his long, sharp hunting knife. As the bear bit down on him, he jabbed the knife into its chest and

26

he pulled it out. Hanging on to the handle as tightly as he could, he jabbed and pulled as hard and as often as he could . . . into the throat, into the chest, even as he felt his scalp being ripped off.

He passed out and was found by his villagers. The bear was dead a few feet from Chow-nie-go's unconscious body. They carried him back to the village. Parts of his hair never grew back, leaving just ugly scars that covered his head, face and body.

Kiachook and her daughters traveled all through the night with hardly any stops. It was only after traveling far, when they could see the familiar hills of home, did their mother say with relief in her voice, "We eat and rest."

Everyone was glad to see the women return safely. Other squirrel hunters had returned; some had come in the day before. The bear had started to rob the snares, sometimes taking both animal and snare.

The skins and meat were hung to dry. Dinner that evening consisted of dry seal meat and dry tomcod because the women were tired and did not feel like cooking. They placed the dry tomcod on a flat rock and, using their stone hammers (thinnish rocks, four to six inches long), pounded the backside of the tomcod, separating the hard dry meat from the bone so it was easier to pull apart. They had picked some greens just before reaching home. Nedercook liked the bittersweet taste these willow leaves left in her mouth.

CHAPTER 5

NEDERCOOK'S ENJOYMENT

It was peaceful in the evening to sit in front of the inne and look out over the Bering Sea. Birds of all kinds were swimming and flying around. Some flew in little groups following close to the shoreline, going west; others were in flocks farther out, while some seemed to be flying around just for the fun of it. Nedercook loved to hear the bird calls along with the gentle sound of the small waves that broke as they rolled ashore. From high in the sky came the distinctive sound of the snipe they called the *kikingatoolic*. It dived earthward, fluttering its wings to make this unusual sound, only to right itself before reaching the ground, quietly fly skyward again until it could make another earthward dive or U-like swoop. It would continue to do this many times during spring courtship. Kiachook looked up and then sang it a special song. Women of her village always sang a song of welcome to the first bird of each species to arrive in the spring. To Nedercook and her mother, hearing this snipe meant spring was really here.

The evening was so still and beautiful that Nedercook walked to the little knoll and sat down just out of sight of the village. The kittiwake gulls were in the process of building their nests on the ledges of the cliffs. They were busy carrying mud and grass from a damp spot about a quarter of a mile inland. They formed two lines. One line was the incoming line, white with little dark markings, streamlined forms flying in the line to the right. They alighted in the mud-grass area, and proceeded to pull and pick up needed material. When they had enough in their beaks they would fly off to join the outgoing line of gulls until they reached the edge of the cliff. From there they would fly to their nests, fastened to the rocks so the high winds and strong rains would not loosen them from the cliff.

Nedercook often marveled at what the birds and animals did, and she was more full of questions than some of the other children. Sometimes when she became too curious and continued with her questions, her mother would look at her and say, "Why don't you ask it?" Nedercook would ponder this and then realize that her mother wished she would study more closely the activity of the bird or animal in question. By watching and listening to the creature, she would find suitable answers.

Nedercook enjoyed the gathering of foods from the various locations. By late spring the willow leaves had grown too old and strong to eat, and the whiter willow shoots she had peeled to eat of the sweet, tender inside had also grown old and tough. Now there was the wild sorrel that grew on the slanting hillsides near to the cliff's edge, along with the wild onions and the sour dock that grew nearby. There were also the greens that grew around the lakes in early spring. Then there were greens that grew above high tide on the beaches. Her mother often mixed these with berries in the late summer and put them up for winter. Nedercook always enjoyed going with her mother to wander in the alder gullies, digging up the tender roots of the big fern. The swarms of mosquitoes that rose from the grass in sheltered spots, swarming around her, humming, biting her, did not upset her. Summer and sunny days had always brought mosquitoes as far back as she could remember, and, as far back as she could remember, they were always biting her. This was part of spring, summer, warm days, and she did not mind too much; she would slap and itch and give it no further thought. Her mother would bring the fern root home to boil in the blood of seal, or oogruk. This was considered a real treat.

Nedercook enjoyed fishing and would go with mother, father or brother if they would take her. Kiachook liked to fish for the wolf fish, a long, eel-like fish with a very large mouth that was filled with long, sharp teeth. For bait her mother would gather from the hillside by the cliffs a root from one of the slender wild plants. She would scrape off the dark outer skin and tie the white root to the hook that was made from bone, horn, or a hawk's claw. This root also attracted another fish that had a big head, but was short and built more like the fish called an Irish lord, only this fish had quiet browns and grayish colors.

Kiachook liked to get up early when she went fishing for wolf fish. If the sea was not too rough Kiachook and her daughter would jump from rock to rock, going out as far as they could to a cluster of rocks which had fallen sometime back, and fish from there. Nedercook did not fish for wolf fish, she carried the stick and bag. Kiachook always insisted they carry a stick to use as a club to kill the fish. She warned her daughter to make sure the fish was dead before trying to pick it up; the teeth were very sharp.

Nedercook knew that a kayak could be used to fish from, but the men were the ones who used the kayaks. The men had given up fishing for wolf fish with kayaks. Long ago, one man who went fishing in his kayak caught a large wolf fish. He hit it on the head and, believing it dead, carelessly put it into his kayak and continued fishing. Apparently the fish was only stunned because, as the man sat in the oval opening of his kayak, the fish recovered and bit off his private parts so he suffered a horrible death. So they fished for wolf fish from rocks now, even though it was a little slower. The dark fish skin was used as a trim on rain parkas and water mukluks, and in any place where a piece of very thin skin was needed. Kiachook liked the meat of this fish very much. After skinning it she would boil a big pot of it and then the family would sit around dipping out chunks to eat with oil and leaves. The fishing season for it was short.

Nedercook liked to walk to the cliffs and then walk along the top near the edge, looking across the Bering Sea. She would take a pack and pick edible greens. Many times she would stop to watch the whales, seals or birds. She often wondered how or why the waves would come rolling so tirelessly in, one after another, repeating. She never tired of this and with the curiosity of a child she wondered why the sea did not get tired.

Forget-me-nots grew in profusion on many of the sunny slopes, making hillsides near her blue. Wild arctic poppies and other tundra flowers added their sprinkling of color and perfume. Bees would fly from flower to flower. Often the breeze from the sea would be enough to keep the mosquitoes away.

Watching the sea parrots standing before their homes on the cliffs and listening to them make their calls and noises, she would often try to mimic them, and the songs of many birds, and the sounds of animals. A little way from shore, two male puffins were in combat on the water. They had been fighting for some time. Often the fight would last until one or the other died, but at times after a long fight, if something scared them, they would both give up. If the puffins could still fly they would, but sometimes one would be too tired so it would swim off. Nedercook liked to see them both live. Later she enjoyed watching the parents bring little fish back in their colorful beaks to feed their young. She never saw the young come from their homes, so she figured they must leave in the dark of night.

CHAPTER 6
EGGS

Each day Nedercook would check to see whether the murres (black and white diving birds) had started to lay eggs. This she could do by looking just over the cliffs at a section where the birds roosted on the cliffs. These sea birds did not bother to build a nest but rather laid their eggs on the bare ledges, or any place on the cliff where the bird could sit. If the mother was not careful and flew off suddenly, the egg would roll off and break as it fell, unless it was over water. On calm days when the water was clear, her father would often go in his kayak and, using a long pole with a little skin basket fastened to the end, scoop the eggs from the bottom of the sea. Sometimes he would even manage to scoop up a crab.

Inerluk thought he was too old to climb the cliffs like his two sons and other young men of the village. Sometimes the young men would use a long piece of rawhide; they would pound a stake into the ground, tie the rawhide to it, and then follow the rawhide over the cliff. They would fasten their parkas securely at the waist and then as they reached the eggs they would slip them in through the neck openings of the parka until it was full. They would then climb back up and unload, going back if there were still more eggs within easy reach. Some of the older men took a break while doing this and cracked an egg or two while still on the cliff, and drank the contents. Usually other able-bodied young men went egg gathering with Nedercook's brothers. And depending upon how far up the coast they were going, some women and children followed along — the women picking the wild sorrel and onions. Egg hunters preferred to go over the cliffs on calm days or during the cool of evening. The days were now so long that the nights never became dark. The sun seemed to barely dip below the horizon before it was coming up again. At this time all the little tundra birds would start their singing, even before the sun was showing.

When the egg hunters returned to the village the older people often drank the uncooked eggs from the shell, but the young preferred to have them boiled.

Nedercook and her mother had a spot a little way up along the cliff where they often went. Kiachook had a pole with many pieces joined to make it long, with a little basket on the end. They would drag this with them. Kiachook would stand at the cliff's edge, balancing against the breeze from the sea, slip her long pole over the edge of the cliff, and scoop up the eggs that were within reach. The murres raised but one young. If they lost an egg at the beginning of the season they would lay another in a day or two; if that one was taken they could continue laying eggs until about the middle of July.

On one of the egg-gathering trips, Kiachook, knowing how young Nedercook liked to participate in the gathering of food, said that she saw a puffin come from a hole not too far from the top of the cliff, and that farther down there might be a gull's nest. Nedercook was excited and wanted to go after the egg, but her mother said, "Next time. We need rope." On these trips they usually picked a bag of sorrel before returning home.

33

Nedercook could hardly wait for the next trip, but on the scheduled day it was stormy and windy. Her mother said, "No good, we wait." Nedercook knew how treacherous the wind at the cliff's edge could be. It would blow you back away from the edge, just when you got braced against it, then suddenly it would whip around, blowing you toward the edge. Either way was bad, and the wind did both, as if wanting you to fall over the edge.

Starting out the next day, Nedercook made sure that the piece of rawhide was in her packsack. Her heart was light as she pulled and dragged Kiachook's long pole over the uneven tundra. Impatiently she sat back a few feet from the cliff's edge, where her mother always made her sit. She watched her mother advance confidently to the edge of the cliff. Getting her feet in a secure position, she would begin sliding the long pole slowly down over the edge until it reached the first egg. She turned and twisted the pole so the egg would roll into the little basket without rolling off the cliff. Slowly, hand over hand, she would bring the pole back and while holding the pole with one hand, remove the egg with the other. She placed it on the ground or in the dried sealskin hunting sack she brought especially for this. Kiachook would repeat this until there were no more eggs within reach of her pole. When her mother started to drag the pole back up away from the cliff, Nedercook could relax and move because her mother was out of danger.

Nedercook took the rawhide rope out of her packsack and her mother tied it around her small waist. Then her mother sat down a few feet from the edge, holding the rope between her hands. Nedercook's spirits were high, she was going to get one or maybe two puffin eggs, and her mother had said that there might be a gull's nest a little farther down. Eagerly and happily she went over the cliff, down a few feet to a narrow ledge which continued at a 45-degree angle slanting down the face of the cliff. The ledge narrowed a few feet farther down, where the cliff above seemed to bulge outward above it. Still farther down it narrowed and crumbled to nothing. Nedercook was too anxious to find the eggs to be cautious. Without hesitation, as soon as her feet touched the ledge, she went down on all fours. In her eagerness she paid no attention to the fact that her head was much lower than her hind end. She proceeded happily to crawl down. Soon finding two whitish puffin eggs, she placed them in her parka. Continuing down she looked for the gull nest, but there was no nest and there were no more eggs. Then she noticed that the ledge had turned and petered out to nothing.

"I'd better go back," she thought as a flicker of panic touched her heart. Then, and only then, did Nedercook realize the mistake she had made. Her knees, hips and feet were higher than her head, and behind her, in the direction she wished to go. She tried to turn so she could look back, but the ledge was too narrow for any such move and the incline too steep. In this very dangerous, awkward and uncomfortable position, her body seemed to freeze. In front the ledge ran out and the cliff fell away, 300 feet down, down to where the breakers, still angry from yesterday's storm, crashed against the rocks. A cold fear started to fill Nedercook's heart, a fear such as she had never felt before. She looked at the moving water far below. In between was the constant movement of hundreds of flying birds: murres, puffins, gulls and cormorants. It was enough to make one dizzy, to say nothing of being in this awful position.

What can I do, she thought, as she called faintly "Mama" in her native tongue. But her mother was too far away to hear her above all the sounds from birds, the breeze and waves. For long minutes she remained in position, feeling very uncomfortable and unsafe. What can I do? kept running through her head. To try to turn would be to fall off the cliff, because she had crawled down under the rocks that bulged outward above her, making her position even more insecure. After a time she thought, maybe I should just jump out and turn around as I do. But then she remembered that there was no peg of wood to hold her, only her mother's hands; with the unexpected weight the rawhide would either slip through them or she would pull them both to their death, crashing on the rocks and waters below. She shuddered and was glad that she had not done this on impulse. No, that would not do, but what? what, she thought, should I do?

She put her head down to her hands as if trying to shut out the sight before her eyes. For several minutes she crouched in this position, her body pressed against the cliff. A calm seemed to fill her mind; her body gained strength and courage. No matter how hard it is, her being seemed to say, you came down this way — now you must go back up.

Slowly, very cautiously, she raised her right knee and foot, since they were the ones nearer the cliff. She kept her leg pressed to the cliff as she inched it up and back. Then ever so carefully she inched the other knee and foot back. Her hands followed. As she did this she noticed that the rawhide tightened ever so gently. Up over the uneven rocks she slowly made her backward way, inch by inch, until she reached the wider ledge. When she neared the top, the ledge was wide enough for her to get her knees in position, and she turned around, facing up the ledge. The rest was easy.

Kiachook looked much relieved as Nedercook climbed back from the cliff's edge. "You all right? I worried, you long time."

When Nedercook removed only two parrot eggs her mother remarked, "Two eggs, too long, don't go down again." Nedercook was not planning another trip anyway — not down there.

Around the evening meal praise was high for her and

for the good flavor of the two special eggs Nedercook had given to her parents. Nedercook was more quiet than usual. She had learned a big lesson this day and, although she did not say anything to her family, her mind brought the experience back to her many times. She was thankful that she had not acted in panic, but had waited for other thoughts to enter her mind. She shuddered at the remembrance that, had she jumped, she and her mother would not be sitting here enjoying the evening meal.

Nedercook often watched the raven during the month of July, at least the first half of the month, when the murres' eggs lay on the cliffs. The raven would fly up from the cliff, where it had stolen an egg, carrying the egg in its beak. He would fly to a spot on the tundra, hop around, then bury the egg, hop around some more, and then fly off to get another. He would bury or hide each one in a different place — sometimes near the cliff's edge, and the next time possibly one-quarter to a half-mile inland. Nedercook tried to locate the eggs a couple of times, but they were too well hidden.

CHAPTER 7

WOMEN OF THE SEA

Nedercook had been told about the "women of sea" who came to Chu-kuk Point during the salmon season. Villagers who had supposedly seen them said there were several women of the sea inhabiting the waters around the point during the salmon fishing season. Often the women of the sea would go fishing in pairs. The women of the sea would always surface to eat the fish. They swam gracefully and all had very, very long, dark hair. The soles of their feet were always extremely white.

The salmon fishing season was nearly there. The people of the village were getting ready to make their annual move farther west along the coast to what they called the summer camp at Magarchumuk. At this location it was easier to set their nets from a nice beach, where the little stream they called Kook-kar-nee brought fresh water down through camp, making the cutting and cleaning of fish easier.

Nedercook knew that the ban on picking green would come any day now, as the willow leaves were already old. She let her mind wander back to when she was very small.

She had wandered off as a little child and eaten of the forbidden greens. Her mother, looking for her, found her with all the evidence of greens around her lips and mouth. She remembered her mother's stricken look, and how she had glanced all around and then hurriedly and carefully wiped away all evidence. She then made her drink water to clean her mouth.

Her mother explained to her in no uncertain terms that the ban was to be observed by all the villagers and their children. Nedercook remembered how much she loved the greens as a child, and how after that she would somehow just happen to wander away, then eat the greens, figuring if she was far enough away from camp it was all right, as long as she wiped her mouth and lips carefully and then drank water. Her mother feared that if the bans and taboos of the village were broken, the one responsible might be put to death, the logic being one death for the safety of the entire village.

Her thoughts returned to the women of the sea. As soon as the Inerluk household settled for the night, Nedercook asked her father to tell her about the women of the sea. Her father said he had not seen any, but that did not mean there were none. He was always too busy during the time of the salmon run, putting up fish to dry for the coming year, to go the many miles it took to look for the women of the sea. Chu-kuk Point was on the west side of Rocky Point. He explained that her mother might be able to tell her better of this, but he knew she was very tired this evening since she had been away all day helping someone who had hurt herself from a big fall. So he would tell her what two of her mother's friends had told her. He went on to say that her mother had played and grown up with these two people before they had married and moved away. "Your mother says," he continued, "that she does not believe that they would tell lies, or be storytellers, so your mother believes what they said."

These two people told your mother of how, one summer they set their gill net out for salmon near the end of a long beach a little west of Chu-kuk Point. They had tied the rawhide from the net to a stick at the end of their skin boat. They had turned their boat over, as was the custom, to let it drain if it had been in stormy water or if it had rained. After setting out the net they sat down to rest and watch the net. It was such a calm day, they could see by the floats if any fish hit the net. Then a short distance away they saw a woman of the sea; she was swimming toward their net. When she came to the net she grabbed it along the top where the floats were fastened to the top line. She followed the net, going hand over hand, until she came to the shore. All the time the two people sat watching, motionless and speechless. She followed the line to the stick. Then she saw the boat and going to it she patted it with her hands, as a drummer would. She did this for quite awhile, going back and forth along the boat. Then the woman of the sea retraced her steps into the water and swam out to sea. The two who were watching said that her hair was very long, extra long and flowing.

CHAPTER 8

SALMON FISHING TIME

Taboos and bans would be in effect until the salmon came. These included, pulling up or picking of green grass, picking any green leaves, and any kind of sewing. The children could run and play and be as active as they liked.

A few days later it was time for the entire village to move to the summer fishing camp in anticipation of the salmon run; they would travel there by oomiak.

Inerluk's spot for his fish net was on the right side of the creek if you looked toward the sea. Here for years he had set his nets. Behind this were his camp and fish racks of Kiachook.

After landing the big oomiak, getting the net into the water was the most important thing. Nedercook ran up the hillside to get the long pole that was stored there and used for this. Her father had joined many pieces very smoothly, and had notched the outer end on which he hooked the end of the net rope. Nedercook and her mother always helped him the first time, keeping the net flowing in to the water untangled and keeping the tension right so it would not slip off the end. Inerluk was so good at this that he could do it alone, but the first time was a ritual they did together. When the pole could be pushed no farther, Inerluk gave it a quick forward push, and then he pulled the pole quickly back. The rawhide slipped off; the net was set. Nedercook pulled the pole above the water line, where it would be safe.

Nedercook liked this hustle and bustle of activity. This year she was old enough to have the responsibility for taking care of the living coals which her father had carefully packed in one of Kiachook's thick clay pots, along with some ashes. Her father said she was old enough to try to start a fire with one coal; she would do this while they carried their belongings to where they would set up camp. Carefully Nedercook carried the pot to the old fireplace. Then she looked along the beach for birch bark and small pieces of dry wood. With two sticks she removed one coal, placing it in the fireplace. Then she moved the pot to a safer place. She tore the bark into small pieces and laid these on the coal; when the bark curled and smoked she began to blow gently. As it glowed and became red she blew a little harder and the bark caught fire; quickly she added more and bigger pieces, then the sticks and larger pieces. She hovered around it until she was sure it would not go out, adding larger pieces of wood as needed. Without her knowledge Kiachook and Inerluk were keeping an eye on her as they worked. "It is going," Nedercook happily announced.

The wise old parents both stopped work and walked near the fire as if they had not been aware of the rising smoke. "You make good fire," they both said in a voice filled with praise. Then her father added, "You want to get cooking wood?" Nedercook liked a fire that was not just coals. She happily gathered wood, piling it between the camp and the fireplace. Wood was plentiful so she gathered pieces of all sizes. She knew that each storm brought a new supply of driftwood.

There was great excitement up and down the beach, where others were setting out their nets and making camp. The salmon run had begun, they knew because every so often one could be seen jumping from the salt water. Nedercook knew that as the run increased there would be lots more jumping. Nedercook liked this summer camp; the shelter was not as comfortable against stormy weather as the inne. The summer house was made by tying driftwood together, then using sea mammal skins on top to shed the rain. More wood was piled around the sides to help keep out the wind. However, in summer, especially at the beginning, most of the days were warm and it was fun. The smoke curled skyward as she looked beyond it to the fish rack her father had built for her mother long before she was born. It too, was close to the clear, fast little stream.

Kiachook asked her daughter if she would put half salty sea water and half fresh water into some of the cooking pots and set them to heat. Her father would soon check the net. Inerluk had been watching the net eagerly. If the fish hit low it would be hard to tell, but if they hit high the smooth, dry wooden floats would bob. Sometimes there would be a splash if a great many hit the net at one time. If too many got into the net the floats would sink. Pulling in the net was exciting; fish were splashing and those that looked like they might get loose were grabbed by eager hands.

This was a good catch; mother and daughter cut up the salmon and filled the cooking pots. They stuck sticks into some from the mouth end and pushed the other ends of the sticks into the sand; thus the fire roasted the fish, which needed only an occasional turning. Nedercook watched the cooking pots and roasting fish while her mother cut and cleaned and hung the other salmon. Kiachook filleted the fish with her stone and bone ulu. Nedercook had learned that boiling fish was easy. Her mother had taught her to keep it boiling, with an occasional stirring, until all the foam disappeared. When this happened she removed the pot from the fire and ran to tell her mother, who left the cutting stand to wash her hands in the stream. Nedercook ran to tell her father and brothers, who had just finished re-setting the net.

All of the family gathered around the fireplace. Solemnly, as most rituals were carried out, each member of the family took a pinch of ashes from the fireplace and each took a taste of ashes. This was done before they could eat of this year's new salmon catch. After this Kiachook quickly dipped out chunks of the fresh boiled fish onto a large wooden platter, sprinkling seal oil over all. Everyone took pieces they liked. The "Umm-mm's" were murmured as they savored the fish, while drinking of the thin broth. Greens and other foods were ignored as they enjoyed the first fresh salmon.

Kiachook took a fin from a piece she had, and passed it to Nedercook, while Inerluk gave another to his older son Nutchuk. Oolark had already taken a piece with the fin attached. The second dorsal fin on a salmon is very small, but it is supposed to help protect the eater from the attack of the dreaded bear.

This was a happy time for the adults, the ban on greens and sewing was lifted, and men whose garments were torn could now have them mended. For the very small children a ban was on: they were not supposed to go around stomping their feet. This ban did not bother Nedercook as she was long past that age group. This ban's only punishment was a reprimand from a parent or anyone who caught the little one doing it.

After this run of salmon was over there would be a break before the other species of salmon would follow, near fall. But this run and the next were very busy times because villagers tried to put up as much during the early runs as they could. This was the best time for drying the fish, with lots of sun, wind, and hardly any rain, so the fish crusted fast, the flies did not get a chance to lay their eggs and ruin them, and the fish dried without mold. Kiachook worked long hours, cleaning and hanging fish. Inerluk and Nedercook put the net in, carried fish up to the cutting stand, and, whenever she could, Nedercook helped cut, fillet, and cut diagonal slashes into the rich salmon flesh so it would dry quicker. She also hung up as many as she could. The rows of eggs from the fish lay over rocks or on logs to dry for storage. As the fish dried they took it from the rack and Inerluk tied it in bundles. He let these bundles hang from the ends of cache poles to dry some more until it was time to store it away.

Kiachook liked to boil the largest salmon heads until the gristle was soft so she could eat it. Some of the smaller heads they scattered to dry, but sometimes they dug a deep hole generally about three feet deep, lined the bottom with grass, and then put in quite a lot of fish heads, filling the hole within two feet of the top. Grass was added and then it was covered with earth, sealing it off until after freezeup when they would find the marker and dig it up, sometimes after snow. Even to the Eskimo who was used to smelling strong smells, this had an odor of its own. Eskimos had a name for it, "Rotten." (One should not attempt this; occasionally the rotten fish heads would poison and kill the eater.) They also dried the center bones that were removed when they filleted the fish to dry. If not fed to the dogs, they were soaked, boiled and eaten. If the weather was cloudy and rainy, Kiachook turned all the fish that was not dry so the skin side was out. The dry ones were stored.

During this time Inerluk set his seal net out when the water was not rough, and sometimes at night it would catch a beluga whale or seal. This brought much happiness.

One type of seal caught was the oogruk (bearded seal). Some of their young that the Eskimos called "the red-faced ones" were feared by men in kayaks. They had a reputation of tipping over kayaks, and men would often drown. If this was done by the animal in play, or if the young were feeling their strength and looking for a challenge, Nedercook did not know, but she hoped her brothers would not meet up with the red-faced one, unless they saw it first and could spear it.

Through the long days of summer the Inerluk family fished and put up salmon. Some days there were not many; on those days the women gathered greens or did other necessary work. Other days, it was work on fish from morning until night, but really there was no real night as the days were still long and light. Each day on any beach Nedercook always looked for flat rocks that might be suitable for plates, or for long, thin rocks to use as hammers when eating dry or hard food. Her father would make wooden bowls, plates and buckets from driftwood, but he did not have much time for this; the few pieces he made were beautifully finished. For years he was proclaimed as one of the best providers of the village; now his sons were fast becoming good hunters, earning their own reputations.

On calm days Nedercook's father and brothers would take the oomiak loaded with the bundles of dry fish and put them in storage at their winter camp.

As the season wore on there would be rainy days and the sea would become rough. Logs would be floating by, so nets had to be taken out or they would be lost.

Nedercook liked the storms of early summer, when the weather was still warm. When it rained and got her wet, it did not make her cold. She liked to walk the beach during and soon after a storm. Always there was new wood, occasionally a dead mammal, some in very good condition that the village used for food. If the dead animals were very old the villagers hung them up for dog food. There were dead sea birds, too; it made her feel sad for just a little while as she looked at them and wondered how they had died.

It was on one of her walks after a storm that she found a piece of wood such as she had never seen before; it was a three-foot by six-inch by two-inch piece of board. Never had she seen anything like this before; it looked so clean, smooth and different. She became excited; she picked it up and ran all the way back to the family camp. It was a curiosity for the whole village. No one had ever seen anything like it. They each held it, rubbed it and marveled and wondered where it had come from, how it was formed so smooth and thin.

During the hot days of summer the old bull walrus would sometimes come to the beaches, flopping up above the water line to sleep and rest. Nedercook was fascinated by the huge animals and she was also a little afraid. If she happened to spot one before her brothers or the other villagers, she would run for her brothers and together they would go with other hunters to kill the walrus.

Seals occasionally came to the beach. Once after the salmon run had slowed down, Nedercook and her mother were walking the beach on their way to check the berries for ripeness. They saw a seal on the beach. Both picked up strong sticks and worked their way between it and the water. Toward the last they had to move very fast but they killed it. "We go back," Kiachook said, and together they pulled, lifted and dragged the seal home. It was a slow trip but they were happy because they had fresh meat, blubber, inner foods such as liver and heart, and a seal poke for the making — or perhaps mukluks, mittens or a packsack.

Now that summer was here, salmon trout, as they called them, came up the streams. When Oolark mentioned going on a trout-spearing trip, his sister wanted to go. After he agreed, he decided that she, too, should have a spear. He picked a willow that had a fork and cut a length he thought she could handle. On the spear end he left two long prongs and sharpened the points as best he could.

They walked upstream carefully checking for trout. As deeper holes came into view, Oolark asked Nedercook to come to the side from which the sun shone. He said her reflection might scare the fish, but he also cautioned her about the shadow she would cast. Holding their crude spears upright, they approached a clump of willows. "No quick move until you are ready to spear fish," Oolark said to his sister. Some trout were swimming about while some remained in one place, with just their fins moving. She saw Oolark's spear ever so slowly descend to the water and continue down. Trying to be as slow and easy as he, she lowered hers.

Oolark's spear stopped a few inches above a large trout. "Now!" he exclaimed, as he plunged his spear down.

Nedercook took only a second to follow but she was too slow. The fish darted away untouched. Oolark's fish came wiggling to the bank, and he quickly killed it. He broke off a branch that had a fork near the end. Picking up the fish, he pushed the small end in behind the gills and out the mouth. In what seemed like no time he managed to get all the fish he wanted. Nedercook had only one, but she did not want it strung on with his. She got a willow and strung hers as her brother had, and proudly carried it home. Kiachook was pleased. She used her ulu to cut and remove the sharp teeth from the top of the trout's tongue; her daughter did the same. The teeth did not soften when cooked and were dangerous to eat.

CHAPTER 9
KILLER WHALE

R ocky Point Eskimos were told early in life, "Never take the life of the killer whale. In return the whale will not strike at the hunter's kayak."

On this beautiful day when Nedercook and her mother were out roaming the hillsides above the cliffs, walking and looking for anything edible, they saw killer whales going by in the sea below. They were all heading westward and all in formation. The smaller whales were closest to the shore; the next size about an eighth of a mile farther out and, beyond that, the big ones. It was quite a sight. It seemed as if the whole sea was alive with whales. Nedercook could hear them surface and dive. She was excited. She had never seen so many large animals in this kind of formation. It was absolutely thrilling to watch the big mammals. As she stood in awe, watching them surface together in long lines, she glanced at her mother's face and saw fear. She did not expect this since they were both on land and the whales could not get them. Kiachook was not afraid for her or her daughter. She was afraid her husband or sons might be at sea in a kayak.

Nedercook and her mother sat on the ground to watch the big animals after they had passed. The late afternoon was quiet and they could still hear the sounds of the whales as they came up and then splashed down out of sight. For some reason Nedercook got up and walked to look down into the water near the cliff. Right next to the beach, just as close as they could get and still be in water, were six beluga whales. Instantly she could

tell that they were terrified. Fear was in their every move; in the quiet way they were sort of sliding along, barely surfacing, their whole bodies showed fear.

"Look, mama!" she whispered as she motioned with her hand.

"Very scared," Kiachook whispered back as together they watched the escaping whales follow the shoreline, away from the path of the killer whales. Looking westward, they saw the killer whales going on.

The scene below reminded Nedercook of another time she and her mother had been out walking. The day was not so calm. The wind was blowing from the southwest. They had spotted two killer whales going west about a quarter of a mile out to sea. Kiachook had spoken. She spoke as one addressing the sky, the sea, the universe. She asked the killer whales to be generous and to share a little of their kill with her and her family, as none of her family had ever tried to harm them. By then the whales had passed them by almost a quarter of a mile. As they watched they saw splashes by the whales and swirly motions, and then there was a small circle of sheen on the water, which appeared darker for a short

time. Nedercook's vivid imagination pictured blood making it so. After awhile the water returned to normal and Nedercook could not pick the exact spot anymore.

"We look at beach," Kiachook said as she turned west. They would climb a little more and then descend to the beach. Then they would walk for a ways before returning. Nedercook knew that if they did not find anything, her mother would be up at daybreak to walk again, and she would be with her. She remembered the piece of beluga whale they had found washing at the shoreline. Kiachook happily ran to it, grabbed it. She remembered how she had helped her mother pull it up onto the beach, and how clean and fresh it looked. It was just as if someone had cut the slab with a sharp knife. Kiachook spoke again as if to the elements, giving thanks and thanking the killer whales for their generous gift. Later in appreciation she would throw something small back into the sea.

Around the tenth of August the women checked the berries more regularly, for soon they would be ripe. One day they picked some low red berries they called the salmonberry; they picked them too unripe to eat raw, but they took them home and cooked them with a little water. Nedercook thought they were delicious — just sour berries and a little water.

Nedercook had a special bucket that her father had made for her years ago. It was of beautiful, smooth wood and very well made. She always took it berry picking. She and her mother and other women of the village went across the tundra with the seal-poke containers, usually picking until they were filled. Nedercook liked picking the salmonberries but by the time the containers were full she was glad to go home.

Later, as other berries ripened, they would pick them as they came across them, all into the same container, all except one — a large berry that grew up high on the hillsides where the black moss berries grew. This one, the villagers called the headache berry. Her mother told her not to pick it and not to eat it, because only a few would give one a headache. Nedercook liked picking the black moss berry and the cranberry. They could be picked "dirty" — they called it "dirty" when leaves and twigs came along with the berries. Then they would try to whistle, because it was supposed to make the wind blow stronger. They would pour the berries from a bucket held a few feet up, and the wind would blow away the leaves as the berries fell into the container.

Chapter 10

BELUGA WHALE

Toward the end of summer the north winds would blow very hard. They would blow little whitecaps out toward the sea, causing the water to recede and expose beaches that were seen only during these extreme winds. During one of these windy days Nedercook and her mother were out picking berries on top of the cliffs. After awhile her mother decided that, since the rocks would be exposed, they should go gather mussels. The mussels clung to the seaweed that clung to the rocks. Nedercook knew her mother would also gather some of the soft edible things that also clung to the rocks. She did not like these too well, maybe because they looked like what her mother called them, "ass holes." She recalled how they would shrink back onto the side of the rock, squirting out a liquid as they did. And they were always so hard to get loose from the rocks.

"We be careful," Kiachook said. The water might return quickly if the wind let up and it would trap anyone under the cliffs. As they descended a beach came into view. It was one they called "the big curve." A stream flowed down and into the center of the big curve, so the beach was more sandy than most. On warm summer days Nedercook liked to wade in the shallow water of this beach and feel the soft sand under her feet; many times she would step on bottom fish and feel them wiggle and dart away. She saw several big, low-circling gulls. Then she saw the two beluga whales. They must have been feeding in close and did not go out soon enough, because now there was a sandbar between them and the sea. They must have been trapped for at least a day. There was not enough water to cover them, and the sand was stirred up around them. The gulls were trying for their eyes.

"You go tell," her mother said, "I stay watch." Nedercook put down her berry-picking equipment and started for camp on the run.

Oolark was nearly a quarter of a mile from camp, starting out to look for game, but he was headed in the opposite direction. Like all the family he was an observer. As he walked he looked in all directions and always covered the area behind him. He saw his sister racing toward camp alone and knew that something was wrong or she would not come running home, leaving her mother in the berry patch. All this flashed through his head as he turned and started racing back to camp. Thoughts of fear for his mother filled his heart as he ran.

Inerluk had just brought his net up above high tide line, because the water had become so shallow the net was folded over. He knew that if he left it in the water it would tangle, and when the tide returned it would be improperly set. He also saw Nedercook shortly after she topped the low rise. He started for the beach camp. Nutchuk was busily working on a broken spear; it was for big game and the flint end had broken off. He did not see her until he saw their father hurrying and glancing in her direction.

"Two whales . . . in . . . little water," she panted, gasping for breath. Then she took a large swallow of water and continued, "Mama watch them."

"Where?" her father asked.

"By the big curve."

Spears were grabbed and rawhide was put in all the packsacks, along with a couple of ulus. Each man carried his own hunting knife. They paused to look at the oomiak and the kayaks but all knew the wind was too strong (without saying so). Everyone ran, walked, and ran some more.

Soon the whales were in sight. Gulls were now picking out their eyes. The men dropped their packs above the water mark and went sloshing through the water. There was hardly any life left in the whales, and the men soon finished what was left. The gulls circled and screamed above them, angry at their intrusion.

Kiachook walked out and spoke her thanks to the elements for this wonderful gift of food.

"What we do?" Nutchuk asked.

Inerluk looked at the two big animals lying in the sandy water, then back to the beach and up to the tide line. "Very far," he said, and they all knew he meant it would be a long pack. Then he looked at the sky and out across the water.

"We tie," he said, "No get away. Water come back, we pull."

Oolark rushed to get the rawhide and Kiachook wanted her ulu. Nutchuk and his father were already cutting places to fasten the rawhide near the head. They also wrapped some securely behind the tail fins.

Kiachook cut off two good-sized pieces from the tail fin. Nedercook helped to carry one. They washed off all the sand, then carried the meat to the big, clean rocks. Kiachook cut off pieces so each could take a piece and cut his own bite-size pieces. By then the men had secured the lines to partly buried logs. Not being cooked, the muktuk was quite chewy. Nedercook preferred it boiled until tender and then she really liked it, but she did her share of chewing, and with her fingers dipped berries from one of the buckets. They felt happy and lucky.

When the wind began to lessen they could see the water returning. It began to wash around the whales. Before long the whales were movable and Nutchuk waded out to push while the rest of the family pulled, bringing them to the edge of the beach. Then Inerluk said to his sons, "Go, get help and oomiak."

Without further word the two sons left. It did not seem long before they came into view paddling the large skin boat. Nedercook hopped around and gathered the berry buckets, to place them just above the water line. As soon as the boat touched the children helped the parents into the boat. While the men were tying the lines to the boat, Nedercook climbed in. The whales were tied so one was a little behind the other. Everyone paddled, including the two young men who had accompanied her brothers, but when the whales began to move, Kiachook sat near the back to watch the lines. Nedercook enjoyed this for she seldom rode on the water.

Feasting around the campfire that evening was something she remembered as she grew older. The sun had set by the time the meat and muktuk were cooked. Her mother used a pointed stick. As the water boiled she would test to see if the stick could be pushed through the muktuk easily — then it would be done, soft, tender, and Nedercook thought delicious!

That evening the air was cooler, but it was not too cold so they sat outdoors. There was low talk with an occasional giggle from Nedercook; some had boiled meat, others ate open-fire roasted meat with muktuk. Each piece of muktuk had curled when it cooked. The two young men who had helped shared the evening meal and were given some of the whale.

CHAPTER 11

FAREWELL, MURRES

Nedercook liked to watch the murres leave the cliffs in early fall, which was about the middle of August.

"Can I go look at murres?" she asked her mother.

"Be careful," her mother replied.

Nedercook walked to the cliffs and sat down near the edge in a spot she often visited. First, during early summer, she would watch the murres as they landed on the cliffs. Sometimes they did not fly up to the cliff properly — due to wind, she figured — for there would be a fluttering of wings, then they would fall back, then land on the next try, to stand calling and bowing their heads. Later their eggs lay on the bare rocks. Still later she would hear the shrill little whistling sounds of the newly-hatched birds. She would see the downy dark-backed, white-fronted little ones; she watched as the parents brought back tiny fish in their black beaks to feed the young, marveled at the fast growth of the ever-hungry young and then soon they were already beginning to leave the cliff! Most of the little ones would stand near the edge or walk to it, if there was a wide ledge, and not show any fear of jumping off the cliff when it was time to leave.

One little one had hatched in a small crevice at the back of a ledge. It seemed timid and seldom left its sheltered home. At times it would walk toward the edge of the ledge, then almost at the edge it would stop, turn around, and run back to the crevice. On other evenings it would walk to the edge, look down, turn quickly and run back to safety, then sit low as if trying to hide.

At this time of the year Nedercook would feel a strange loneliness as she watched and listened to the murres. It seemed as if they were saying "Good-bye" to her, the cliffs and to all of Alaska. The little ones were coaxed by the parent to come and jump from the cliff. She watched as a parent seemed to talk to the young, then walk the few steps, jump off, and fly away. She watched the little brave ones walk to the edge, stand a moment, then jump while their little featherless wings, still covered with down, fluttered as they dropped to the waters far below, disappeared with a splash, then surfaced and always, she marveled, they could swim. Some would go around in little circles at first, but a parent would soon land close by and call. The little one usually stopped the idle swimming and went to the older bird, who seemed to praise it, then turn and swim out toward the far horizon of the Bering Sea, with the little one following in its wake.

She saw another small bird make the jump to the water and come up swimming in circles. The parent bird went to it and then started swimming south, but the little one did not follow; it seemed content just to swim around. The older bird tried again; still the little one swam about as if enjoying this new experience. Then Nedercook saw other murres go to the little one, making sounds, pecking at it. In seconds the parent came and drove off the other birds. Then there was another talking to the young, and this time it obediently followed the older one to sea.

Nedercook felt real pride in all the little birds' achievements as they jumped, but also a real sadness as she watched them head out to sea, because she knew she would not see nor hear them again until after the long, cold winter had passed. She wondered how many would live to return. As darkness descended the gentle murmur of the waves could be heard, but above it all was the roar from the multitude of murres calling to their young. The loners seemed to carry a note of sadness in their voices as if saying good-bye. Nedercook felt like crying as she watched the birds. She knew that tomorrow the spot they had claimed as home during the summer would be bare, and remain so until the cold winter had passed. She looked again at the little timid one, saw it walk to the edge, turn, and run back. She felt for this little one.

Farther westward, one little murre jumped and she saw it land on the rocky beach. The little ball of down scrambled toward the water, but the big gull was faster. It swooped down and pecked it to a stop. Then two of the big gulls fought over it and greedily they gulped it down. As used to death as Nedercook was, she felt helpless, wanting to help the baby bird, but she could only watch it being cruelly devoured. Yet inside she knew it was the way of life. She looked back to the timid little one and saw it rise as its parent came to light on the ledge. The older bird was bending its neck and making sounds; it walked to the edge and jumped off, leaving the little ball of down. It was starting to get dark and Nedercook was hoping to see the little one jump. Slowly it walked to the edge, paused a moment, then jumped, little wings fluttering, to hit the water with a splash and disappear for a few moments. She was glad the drop was to the water, so the hungry gull would not get it. The timid little bird came to the surface and started to peep and swim in circles, but soon the parent bird, which had been flying in circles, came splashing down to land nearby. It seemed to communicate with the little one. Soon the little bird stopped going in circles. As the older bird swam out into the gathering dusk, the little dark figure was right behind. A part of Nedercook felt sad while the other part felt proud in a strange way. The little one had found courage enough to jump, and had escaped the gull, which kept flying around watching for any small bird that might land on the beach.

Soon it would be dark. Nedercook would have liked to stay until she could not see any more, but she decided to go home before her parents became worried. She knew that very soon the nights would not be filled with the cry of the murres, and gone too would be the warm summer evenings. The puffins were leaving, but she decided that they must go during the dark because she never saw any leave — they just disappeared. Once she had found a baby puffin washed up on the beach. Its body was covered with black down. Some of the puffins made holes in the earth, much like some swallows, just above the rocks near the top of the cliff; others nested in deep cracks in the rocks of the cliff. She liked to mimic the call of the puffin as it stood outside its home. She also liked to mimic the calls of different birds and animals.

CHAPTER 12
COLDER NIGHTS

K iachook and her daughter would often walk the
beaches to look for anything to salvage, and for
the long, dead roots that grew from the stumps
of the big, dead trees that washed up on the beaches after
a storm, some coming from as far away as the Yukon
River. These dry roots were used on dark nights
whenever a torch was needed, as to go to look for
something in the storeroom. The end of the root was

dunked into seal oil and then lit from the seal oil lamp or from the fireplace, and carried to where it was needed. The seal oil lamp, as a rule, was not carried about — it was too valuable.

As fall approached, the camp was moved back to the village, along with all the food they had gathered and put up for the winter.

With the coming of the big harvest moon in September, the ban on spinning their primitive tops was lifted and the children were happy. On clear nights, when the moon was at its fullest, all the villagers would come outside. They would all keep their faces looking up to the moon, and all would howl for a short time.

Wild cotton was gathered during these dry, cool days and put in storage. It was used to catch the sparks of flint if one needed to start a fire, and to plug the ears of children when they had to sleep away from home on the tundra, especially during spring. During this time the women also gathered the big, rusty-colored moss which seemed to grow best in damp places. It was used for wicks in the seal oil lamps. This moss was also used between the baby and the skin (a piece of dehaired seal or caribou skin) that served as a diaper. Moss was also used by women who were having their menstrual period. A skin triangle was sewn with a slight pucker in which to cradle the moss.

Nedercook's father was good at making the sharp bone tool used for shredding basket or beach grass so it could be used for towels. Pulling the tool down the length of the grass would shred it into very long thin strands. This grass towel was prized and not wasted or used to wipe up just anything; it was special. They called this grass "basket grass." (It is also called beach grass, salt-water grass, rye grass and *Elymus arenarious L.* It grows near salt water from the Aleutian Islands to arctic Canada.)

Freezing nights soon turned the grass to a light gold.

Nedercook and her mother would gather bundles of the dry grass. Nedercook was careful not to let it slip through her hands as she pulled it, because she had cut her hand doing that last year. Today they were pulling only the grass, leaving the root. Last year she and her mother had needed some before the grass had seasoned. They picked it root and all, and hung it by the inne with the root end up to dry. From this grass she and her mother would make baskets, rugs, and containers to store the wild Eskimo potato for the winter.

The nights were cold now. It was beginning to freeze and the moonless nights were very dark. This was the time of year when Nedercook and her mother would walk the beach at dawn. The tomcod washed up onto the beach at night in considerable numbers and froze. Some would still be alive and washing about at the water's edge. They did not wash ashore during the day. Nedercook thought the fish were chased ashore by the feeding whales and seals. Very rarely did they find a real cod, but occasionally they did. Kiachook strung the tomcod up to dry. If the weather got too cold before the fish dried it did not matter. This fish could be boiled while it was partly dry. This was considered a treat with oil.

The livers of the tomcod were saved because they were fatter at this time of the year. Kiachook put the livers in a pot with just a little water and boiling them very slowly, using a wooden stick to stir. She would break the livers up as they cooked, stirring and stirring until the livers coated the stirring stick. Then the mixture was removed, cooled, and black moss berries were added. Nedercook loved the flavor of this dish and the crunch of the berries. She always looked forward to this fall treat.

Snow would soon be here so Kiachook decided the Hudson's Bay tea should be picked. After it was dried, a little was put into boiling water and steeped to

Kiachook's desired strength, then was sipped and enjoyed. Nedercook took a bag from Oopick so she could pick some for her. Nedercook, her family and others of the village helped Oopick whenever they could.

The north winds blew so hard they began to expose the rocks where the mussels clung and the other one she did not like. Many of the villagers gathered these. When they returned Nedercook made a fire outdoors. She knew the weather would soon be too cold for this. As the family sat around the fire that evening, the stars seemed very big and close in the sky. The wind still blew but the village was sheltered from the north, so it was just gusty little winds that stirred the fire.

Next morning her mother said, "We dig roots." So Nedercook put the crude pick-like tools into their packs. Kiachook cut some dry fish into small pieces and put it into her pack. When they reached the head of the little draw they were following, it spread to a flat, grassy area with tussocks scattered here and there.

"We get mouse roots," Kiachook said, so she and Nedercook started walking around where it was evident the mice of the tundra lived.

Nedercook soon felt a soft spot under her mukluk-clad foot. "Here," she called.

Kiachook carefully loosened a small section in a curve that followed the mouse's storage room; it was packed tight with the crooked little brown, nut-like roots of a grass that grew there. Kiachook, using her hand, removed some and put it into her pack. Then she took some of the fish pieces, refilled the storage space, and carefully recovered it, placing extra cover along the edge they had opened. They did this to several of the storage places before moving on up to the hillside to dig for the Eskimo potato, which Kiachook called mat-chew. (Mat-chew, *Hedysarum alpinum*, is known to some Eskimo groups as mashu, or muhzut. Other names are licorice root, bear root and Indian potato.)

"Be very careful when you look at the tops," Khiachook explained to Nedercook. "Do not dig for this one." She showed Nedercook the dried foliage of a plant *(Hedysarum McKenzie)* that looked much like the one they were gathering. "This one is wee, or the husband plant. It is not good and it may kill one who eats it."

They had fun digging for the roots, exclaiming when they found extra large ones. They wandered about on the hillside digging and, as always, watchful for the dreaded bear. At the end of the day they returned with full packs. Nedercook washed some roots of both kinds to add to their dinner, while her father packed the excess into the old grass containers that were made for this use. He buried the bags in holes dug in the stormy-day room, covering them with sand and earth. As they gathered more he would do the same, until they had their winter's supply.

On this particular night Nedercook was watching the lights in the northern sky, something she liked to do before the nights became too cold. Usually the pale, green-white light would dance about the sky, brilliant here, then fading to appear a little farther on, coming and going as if by magic. Sometimes the lights stayed in one place for quite a few minutes, shimmering and dancing about. Tonight was different. The lights were a deep red, something she had never seen before. Why does it change to red now, thought Nedercook. When she could not stand it any longer, she rushed into the inne to ask her parents.

"There is an old saying," her mother replied, "It says that the lights are red when the blood of man has been spilled."

Satisfied, she ran out to watch. Her parents soon joined her. As she watched her mother remarked, "It is said that if one whistles, the lights are supposed to jump more." A shooting star fell, burning brightly, only to fade and be seen no more. Nedercook wondered about it, as she wondered about the many stars.

The cold north winds blew hard, tearing off dead, dry leaves, leaving the alder and willow stripped bare. Until snow came there was no cover for the large tundra hare and the ptarmigan. Both had turned white for winter so they stood out sharply against the brown tundra. Nedercook, standing on a hillside and looking across a gully, could see the white hares as they huddled at the base of an alder bush. The ptarmigan flew or walked in great white flocks on the tundra. She liked this time of year. She would go downwind and creep up to the tundra hares. The wind rustled the dry leaves, creating sounds to cover hers. The big snowy owl also came at this time to sit on the tundra; from a distance it looked big and white, much like a large hare.

Nedercook looked foward eagerly to the coming of the first snow, because this was the time set for Tooogom-ark. This was one evening chosen by the elders to fall, if it could, on the night before the first snow. This was for all the young people of the village. Tooogom-ark meant going from house to house. Nedercook had gone in previous years but this would be her last year to participate.

"You be too old next year," her mother said. She looked forward to this, the last year, she would go with the children.

Beginning at the end of the village and stopping at all of the innes, Nedercook carried the little wooden plate her father had made for her years ago. She knew that some of the children, especially the poorer ones, would take a seal's stomach for a bigger container to put the little gifts in.

For years she had wondered why her mother had always taken food cut into small pieces to Oopick's home on this day — tonight she knew.

Nedercook and the children stopped at old Oopick's. Oopick had a container near and passed a small piece to each child. Nedercook's plate already had pieces of dried tomcod, salmon, meat, dabs of berries, pieces of cooked meat, or whatever the people of each inne had to place upon her plate or put into the children's bags.

Nedercook liked this evening because the children had no taboos and they were not cautioned to be quiet. There was a feeling of real friendship among the group. It did not start snowing until sometime during the night on this, her last Tooogom-ark. She was glad.

She carried her treasures home and gave some to her parents, who were sitting around the glowing coals. It brought her happiness to share her gifts with her parents.

CHAPTER 13

WINTER STORM

With the coming of winter the snows began to fall and the cold winds blew over the area of Nedercook's village, a cold, forlorn piece of windswept land in winter. As the cold spread over this barren land it froze the Bering Sea, as it did the tundra.

On days when the weather was a little warmer, the wind sometimes blew from a southerly direction, bringing with it heavy snows. Snow and wind would stop for only a day or two or three, and then the cold north wind would blow again. It would blow so hard it blew the new-fallen snow into the air, causing a blizzard so dense that Nedercook could not see the little knoll above the inne, or any of the rest of the village. The wind carried the snow along over the barren tundra, piling it in hard drifts in the little creeks where alder and willow grew, and around doorways of the innes. It piled the hard, drifted snow in shapes as if a sculptor had carved great statues in the gullies that emptied into the sea. When the wind stopped the snow was drifted so hard the villagers easily walked on top. Their oogruk-soled mukluks made crisp noises.

One morning Inerluk was checking over the light-weight sinew net he had recently made especially for ptarmigan. It had taken many pieces of sinew tied in many places. He had learned long ago to store sinew and rawhide out of reach of mice and other animals. Today he and his sons were going up the little creek to the right of the village to try for ptarmigan, because one of his sons had seen a large flock there when returning home the day before. Being wise in his primitive way, he had not disturbed them. When Nedercook realized what they were going to do, she asked to go along.

"Long walk," Nutchuk said, "Maybe you get tired and someone have to pack you home." Then his eyes took on a twinkle as he added, "Or leave you."

Nedercook turned to her father, "Can I go? I can help." He nodded his consent.

After walking over a mile they could see some ptarmigan feeding on the willows, so they detoured a half-mile to the left and walked parallel to the little creek until they were opposite the birds. Then they changed direction so they would reach the creek about a half to a quarter-mile above the birds.

Inerluk quickly sized up the creek and picked a place where the willows stopped and left an open space for about a hundred feet in the center. It was here the creek narrowed and then started to widen again. He chose the upper edge of the opening and, motioning as to where the net should go, he and Nutchuk quickly started to set it up. They hooked or looped the top edge over thin branches where they could, and removed other branches so it would be relatively open in the net area. There would be just enough willows to support the net. Nedercook and Oolark quickly tore off branches and started a crude fence to run from the end of the net out in an angle, so it would be like a large V with the net set in the middle. Hurriedly Inerluk checked one side of the fence while Nutchuk checked the other, adding a bit of willow here and there. No one spoke. All was done as quickly and quietly as possible.

Then Inerluk motioned with a wave of one arm. All quietly headed out the way they had come until they reached the point opposite the ptarmigan, which were making feeding noises. Inerluk stopped. He pointed to a spot about a quarter of a mile below the flock. They went in this direction until they reached the creek.

"Now, we make ourselves known," Inerluk said, but added, "We go slow." He looked at Nedercook as he spoke. "We do not frighten the birds or they will fly too soon," and he continued, "we will talk so they can hear us; they will try to walk fast enough to keep ahead of us." Nedercook figured she had better contain her excitement and not rush ahead. They all moved up the creek at a brisk pace. When the birds were getting close to the net, Nedercook was tense with excitement. Finally they came to the open space. Now the birds were hurrying along the fence, with the majority a few feet in front of the net.

"Now!" Inerluk yelled, and they rushed forward, shouting and waving their arms. The flock began to run for a take-off, but they became entangled in the net. Inerluk and his children caught as many as they could. They all knew how to kill the birds quickly, but doing this was not killing for sport; it was for survival. When this was over Inerluk looked at the sky to the south and said, "It will snow, we will not leave the net." Nutchuk started to free it on one end while his father did the same on the other. Oolark and his sister began to gather up the ptarmigan.

The excitement made Nedercook's steps light and she enjoyed the walk home. She did not have to be quiet, so she talked and hopped about. The snow on the tundra was drifted in most places, so tightly packed that she could walk on it without breaking through. She liked this walking on the tundra away from the creek and the willows that tried to tangle up her feet. Later in the winter as the snow became deeper, the creek would be fun; most of the willows would be covered and the drifts would be big and hard. She could stand on a hard, drifted peak and feel tall as she looked down on her surroundings or she could go down to the bottom of one of the many hard-drifted dips and she would be so short that she could see only the snow and a few willow tops.

When they neared home her father grunted his permission for her to run ahead. Her mother and sister were both inside, sitting on the floor with their legs stretched straight out in front of them, a position they sat in when they were sewing. They sat on the grass mats near the center of the inne, making use of the dim light from the skylight above. Paniagon had her material spread out about her on the matt. She was sewing a strip of fancy work to go onto a squirrel parka. She had come to her mother's home to do this, as she often did. For a passing second, Nedercook wondered how her sister could spend so much time on such a tedious task. All the little pieces had to be cut and then sewn together by hand. (It never occurred to her that the bone needle, the hand-twisted sinew, the hard skin thimble and the stone knife were all primitive and slow.)

Kiachook looked up from where she was sitting. Her smile was that of a genuinely happy woman. Her graying hair was parted in the center and braided in one braid that hung down her back. In her lap was a large wooden bowl her husband had carved from a burl that had washed up on the beach. Her left hand held it in place; with her right she was making large circular motions. Her hand served as a spoon and beater as she creamed

71

together seal oil, melted caribou fat, and the meat from cooked lingcod. The bones had been removed and the meat squeezed as dry as possible. Mixing, mixing and mixing it together with just an occasional drop of cold water, she would continue to do this until it became very light and fluffy. The beating of it with her hand took quite a long time and, once started, she would not stop until it was finished. When she was satisfied with its lightness she sometimes added just a little more water, and then, at the very last, she would add some black moss berries and the Eskimo ice cream would be finished.

Nedercook was excitedly telling her mother and sister of the hunt when her father and brothers entered. Paniagon set aside her sewing but Kiachook remained where she was. She beamed her happiness as she looked at the birds they spread onto the skin of a seal used for this purpose. The skin could be cleaned relatively well by wiping it, and it kept the blood from the mat. To her husband's questioning look Kiachook said, "Oopick come. She thankful for seal we sent yesterday," then, after a few more circular motions with her right hand, "She bring caribou fat, sinew and berries."

Inerluk smiled and dipped a finger into the bowl. "No, not finished," Kiachook said.

Paniagon started to pick the ptarmigan, so Nedercook took a place beside her and, placing a bird on her lap, took hold of a few of the body feathers. Using her right thumb and forefinger, she held them firmly as she pulled gently back. Then she moved her hand quickly forward and up in a strong movement. This pulled out whatever feathers she was holding. Her movements were always fast and soon she had a bird clean of all but the long tail and wing feathers. She had even picked the neck and head, because she knew they too would be boiled along with the rest of the bird. Her sister pulled out the long, stubborn tail and wing feathers.

The men went outdoors, but the women knew they would be back to eat when darkness came. Paniagon decided to leave before it got too dark. She would take some of the ptarmigan with her to cook for Kimik and herself.

Everyone gathered inside this evening to eat. It was getting windy outdoors. The pots were full of boiled ptarmigan with the thin broth, a bowl contained leaves preserved in oil, and cleaned Eskimo potatoes along with some from the mouse's root store, cooked, and there was a big bowl of Eskimo ice cream. It seemed like feasting time to Nedercook. The fire was down to glowing coals. Although it was windy, it was not the type of blizzard that prevented them from cooking in the big room. A feeling of love, shared by a caring family, happy laughter and a few words now and then, mingled with the sounds made by people tremendously enjoying their food, filled the inner room that evening.

When bedtime came, little Nedercook had to walk over to the logs by the wall for one last look at all the little pieces of sinew that Paniagon had so painstakingly taken from the ptarmigan before she had put them on to cook. They were spread on the logs to dry separately, all so small. Nutchuk volunteered to close the skylight on his way to bed at the Big Dance House. After she had tucked herself into bed Nedercook asked, even though she knew that her father was tired, so she asked it in a small voice, "Tell me a story?"

"If I can stay awake that long," he replied. She remained silent while he prepared for bed. "This will be one from Cliff Village. We will get our clay near there next spring." Then he began:

> Two men, an uncle and his nephew, left the little village called Cliff. They were going as traveling companions. They walked to the top of the Big Mountain.

They looked down the cliff's edge to the beach several hundred feet below and saw a freshly killed seal.

It was too steep and too far down to get to without a rope. They had no boat or kayak, so they just looked and then said, "What a waste of food down there."

They decided to go on. Finally they came to where the land sloped to the beach and there they found a cave. They went into this tunnel-like cave and followed it for quite awhile, then the tunnel became bigger and the opening higher. They could see a woman sitting. She looked angry. She did not say anything, she just looked angry. Turning her head, she reached for what seemed like her ulu and she threw it at them.

These two men carried their magic charm, and with it they immediately changed into long human hairs. They began to wiggle their way back until they felt it was safe to become human figures again. Then, as quickly as they could, they left the cave. They continued on their way, singing of the narrow escape they had with the woman.

Later they came to the first little cliff that is down below Cheercook. This time they saw a freshly killed spotted seal lying on the beach, but they could not get this one either . . ."

Then little Nedercook heard only the even breathing of her father, and finally his gentle snoring. Part of her was sorry he had fallen asleep before the story was over, and another part of her was glad that he was resting.

Next morning about six inches of snow had fallen. The wind was blowing hard from the southwest. It swirled around the village, stirring up a flurry of snow here and there. By the time the Inerluk family had finished a cold breakfast it was blowing a gale and loose snow seemed to fill the air. It was what they called ung-ul-ik-took, meaning a wind-from-the-south, and beck-cheek-took, a blizzard.

Nedercook had seen storms like this before and knew what they could do. They would make the salt water overflow the ice along the edge of the shore. The sea ice would be pushed in toward the beach, the force causing it to break in places. It would continue to move slowly shoreward, forming large piles of broken ice called pressure ridges. Several pressure ridges would result from this storm. Everyone in the village stayed close to home.

Inerluk peeked out the inne doorway, then quickly closed the skins. He put on his parka and pulled the drawstring close around his face, tied a belt securely over his parka at the waist, and checked to see that the tops of his mukluks were closed snugly. He picked up four of the long, flat rocks his family had gathered through the years, and he tucked them under his left arm, then made his way out of the inne.

The strong wind tried to blow him off balance but, although he was old in years, he was not weak. He carried the rocks to the skylight and laid them next to those already there. This was extra insurance, to keep the skylight cover from becoming loose and tearing or, worse yet, blowing away. The skylight had to be open on days when there was a fire for cooking, so it was just placed over the opening and weighted down. A piece of rawhide attached it to a heavier rock that was left in place to the side. If it came loose, the storm would pour snow into their home and onto the bedding. Replacements took time to make, so Inerluk took no chances. He checked it carefully.

"Bad storm, can't see village," he exclaimed as he brushed away the snow that clung to him upon his return.

During the daylight hours, which seemed darker than most, Inerluk worked at making some fishhooks. He had little sharp bones, sinew, thin rawhide, and one sharp claw of a falcon left from the bird they had found washed up onto the beach last summer. Later he would work a bit more on a herring net he had started.

Kiachook cut a pair of soles large enough for Inerluk,

and then she sat on her grass mat away from the better light, dim as it came through the snow-matted skylight. She did not need light for chewing straight, even crimps into the oogruk-skin soles; she had done this for years, until it became more of a feeling of line and shape. She had crimped so many in the past that her front teeth were beginning to wear flat. Later she would twist sinew for another day's use.

Nedercook tried to do a little sewing, but her stitches did not come out straight and even, like her sister's. They were more like her mother's stitches, stronger and bigger than Paniagon's. She soon gave it up and decided to braid a thick grass rug to go under her father's caribou sleeping pad. Her mother had suggested that he should have a new one, as his had worn thin. Nedercook's brothers and sister did not come. There would be no travel on such a day as this. She was glad they did not have to do any cooking, because they would have had to use what her parents called the stormy day room. It was the little room just off the entrance tunnel as one entered the inne. It had heavy skins covering the doorway and Nedercook remembered how smoky it got the last time they had used it, even though the skins were kept closed about the door. Dinner would be dried food tonight. She was glad to stop working. She got her plate and stone hammer. She looked at the long, slim stone and remembered the sunny day of beachcombing when she had found her very own hammer.

After her parents had gone to bed she lay in hers and listened to the wind, blowing above their home. Then she thought papa is not tired today, so she said, "Papa tell me a story, a long, long story." (Rocky Point Eskimos did not have the word "please" in their vocabulary. They had such words as "excuse me," "did not mean to," and "if you would," but their voices also conveyed much meaning when they spoke, transmitting much feeling in the way a word was said.)

"You want a story?" her father's voice questioned. Then she heard a chuckle and knew that he remembered falling asleep last evening. He began the story:

Once there was a village and in this village lived a rich man and his wife. They had one daughter and she had many suitors. Her father thought that she should marry one. But she said she did not love any of them and she did not want to marry just to be married.

He got mad at her for saying this and drew from his pocket a little homemade knife. (Knives in those days were very scarce.) This he threw to his daughter as he said, "If you do not wish to get married, here, this can be your husband."

Her feelings were deeply hurt. She picked up her little bucket and filled it with bite-size pieces of food. Each piece was just enough for a mouthful.

Then she went to the edge of the sea and stood there wondering which way she should go. Something about the westward direction was stronger, so she started out into the night, headed west. From her wooden bucket she ate only two mouthfuls of food a day, just enough to keep her alive. After much travel she saw in the distance a cliff. When she finally reached it her food supply was gone.

After awhile she saw a cave and decided to enter it. She traveled and traveled for miles and sometimes the rocks under her feet sounded strange, so she would stoop and put one into her bucket. She felt weak and tired, but somehow she kept going until she saw what looked like a star far ahead. After traveling for a long time she saw that it was not a star, but rather light from the other end of the tunnel.

She came out of the tunnel into bright sunlight. She built a very crude shelter using driftwood from the beach. She had no pillow so she used a stump for one, and went to bed. When she awoke it was daylight. She saw a shadow moving and thought it was a man, but it was only her rain parka. She had hung it to dry the night before. She had placed it on a stick beside her shelter, saying to herself, "I do not want anyone disturbing me even though I have only a driftwood pillow."

Looking down toward the beach, she saw a freshly killed spotted seal. She used her father's knife to cut and clean the seal. Oh! this was food, and lots of it, she ate well.

Then she looked out toward the tundra, thinking there may be berries, so she took her little wooden bucket and went forth. She found some berries and started picking. While she was doing this she came upon a freshly killed caribou. Using her father's knife again, she cleaned it, cut it and hung the meat to dry but saved some for her dinner.

This strange appearance of freshly killed game continued as the days passed. One morning she was looking out to sea and saw something shining on the water. It was a kayak and it was coming from the sea straight toward her. When it touched the beach the man called her by name and asked her to come down. He told her to crawl inside the kayak. (If one is not familiar with this, it is dark inside because there are no windows; the man sits in the one hole near the middle with his clothes pressing against the sides.) She decided that since she was alone and did not have anyone to help her, she would go with him.

He told her not to open her eyes, or try to look around in the kayak; however, temptation was too great and she opened her eyes and saw a clear, blue sky. The man immediately told her that he had said she was not to open her eyes. She closed her eyes as he spoke.

They landed on an island and he said, "My home is up there. Go up there but do not cook, as I am going to get us some fresh food." It was a typical old house. In no time the man came to the house bringing with him a spotted seal, so they proceeded to prepare food from it. Every day after that he would go out hunting and bring home a fresh seal for their food.

He kept filling her with food, and then one evening as they were caressing, she noticed the way he pinched her on the arm and then put his fingers to his mouth, just as if he were tasting her.

Next morning as soon as the man had gone to hunt, a handsome stranger came to the skylight. He told her to come out and to hurry up about it. He led her down a little bank and showed her a big pile of human bones.

78

Some of the bones still had ladys' bracelets attached to them.

"See," he said, "this is the way you too will soon end." He then asked her if there was a certain kind of seal that would keep the hunter away for the longest time. She told him there was a certain kind of spotted seal. The stranger warned her not to tell the man she had seen anyone, just ask him to get her the seal.

When the man returned home he asked right away, "Who have you been talking to at the skylight?"

"No one," she said, then she thought a moment and said, "Oh! yes, I was talking to a fly that was at the skylight because I used to see them at my home."

"And you said that you were not talking," he grumbled. That evening he started to pinch her more earnestly than he had before. She said, "Leave me alone, because tomorrow I want to have a big feed of seal." Then she named the hard-to-get seal.

When he heard the name of the seal, he sat motionless for some time before saying that the one she asked for was quite difficult to get, but he would try.

As soon as the hunter left the next morning the handsome stranger appeared and told her to hurry. She followed him to a little knoll some distance from the house. Reaching it, she saw a large eagle skin. He told her he would go inside of the skin, and she should climb on its back, but to keep her eyes shut.

Just as they were leaving the ground she heard something and opened her eyes. There on the water below was a huge loon, flapping its wings as it tried unsuccessfully to leave the water.

"That's my wife, bring her back." called the loon. The eagle spoke, saying, "That was your husband," and a moment later he continued, "Look at that bunch of floating driftwood, that was your home with him." (The loon mentioned in this story is supposed to be what the Eskimos called a *yaark-cha*, the biggest loon-like bird known to the villagers. It is believed nonexistent now. It resembled a penguin.)

The stranger continued to fly toward the highest mountain where they landed on the rocks near the top. There he motioned to a little house and told her to enter it, as his mother and father were inside. He would be

80

right back, as he was going to get a caribou for dinner.

She entered to find an elderly couple and a young woman who looked like she was from Diomede Island.

The old folks were talking softly to each other, wondering where their son had found this new woman. When he returned with the caribou they all ate and there seemed to be much joy. Even the young woman from Diomede seemed happy.

Next day the two young women were looking down into the valley and wondering if one of the benches (flat area) might be a good place to pick salmonberries. They cut a hide into strips to make rope. Tying it together, they went down the rope one at a time, until they passed the steep cliff of the mountain. They left the rope hanging and proceeded on foot.

The berries were luscious and everything else was forgotten but the present joy of picking berries. Suddenly they were startled by the flapping of wings, and they saw a big eagle coming down fast. It landed beside them. Then they heard the voice of their friend, the eagle, as he said, "Oh my, I nearly killed you by mistake. From up there I thought that you were a couple of caribou. After this if you are going to leave the house, tell me first and I will fly you wherever you wish to go."

That evening the two women made Eskimo ice cream from the caribou fat and some of the berries they had picked. They gave the elder eagles a bowl each. At first they tasted it very gingerly, but they soon decided they liked it very much.

For some reason the eagle took the Diomede woman back to her island.

Then as time passed the woman with her father's knife and the eagle became the parents of two sons. The eagle caught an expression of sadness on his wife's face one evening and asked her what was wrong.

"I am thinking of my home, mother and father," she said.

"That is easy, we will go and see them," he replied.

He got two dead trees and tied some strong but light branches in the center so she would have a place to sit, then he built a shelter around it to protect her from the elements. He then added quite a lot of food for the trip and to share with her parents.

She described where she once had lived, because he wanted to make a landing some distance away and go the rest of the way on foot. When they were ready to leave she entered the shelter. He told her to keep her eyes closed, which she did, but after awhile she could not stand it any longer and opened them. On either side flew two little eagles each holding onto the ropes attached to the dead tree, about where her chair was, and in front flew the big father eagle, pulling her through the air. The eagle landed a short distance from the village.

When the entered her parents' home she said, "I am your daughter, I have been married, but I have come back to visit you."

In those days there was a men's section at the Big Dance House where visiting men could stay. This was where bachelors of the village stayed and visiting men. Her husband stayed there. She and the children stayed with the parents. One day as she was preparing food to take to him she accidentally overheard her parents talking.

"This surely is not our daughter for she must be dead. So this must be an impostor who is taking advantage of us."

Just as before, the hurt returned deep and painful, so she told her husband, who said, "We can leave if you want to."

She wanted to leave, so they prepared to go. When they were ready, and just before she walked out of the door, she stood before her father and said, "I am your daughter, even though you do not believe me."

Reaching into her pocket, she pulled forth the little knife that he had thrown at her years ago, and as she threw it to him she said, "Since you refuse to believe I am your daughter, here this can be your daughter."

The old folks immediately recognized the knife and, with tears in their eyes, begged her to stay, but she left with her husband and sons, returning to their home on the mountain. As the old legend goes, they lived there happily ever after.

When her father finished telling the story, Nedercook lay listening to the noises of the storm, happy that her father had not fallen asleep tonight.

Life continued much the same, with variations in work that could be done indoors. On the third evening, after Inerluk had finished a story, he added, "Maybe no storm tomorrow."

CHAPTER 14

BIG BLACK DUCK

When Nedercook awoke next morning the first thing that she became aware of was the absence of the noises the wind made. She realized that she was alone in the inne. Dressing quickly, she hurried outdoors; as she did, she noticed the entrance had been cleared of snow. A few feet from the doorway she stopped to look about.

The early morning light coming across the frozen Bering Sea was beautiful. It made the pressure ridges stand out against the low backlight. The snow had drifted in hard, sculptured lines which caused light and shade. The village was clearly visible and alive with people, children running here and there, adults in and out. Some were cleaning the snow away from their entrance ways.

Nedercook reasoned that her family was also in the village checking on family and friends. She took off on a run. She found her father at old Oopick's. He was clearing away the snow. She helped and it was soon finished. Then they decided to return home and have something to eat. They were joined by Oolark and Nutchuk. The men were deciding what to do. Hunting after a big storm was usually good, they figured, but where was the best place to go today? Should they go near the Iknutak Mountain, where the caribou would have gathered in the lee side during the big storm (caribou lived in this area then), or out onto the ice in search of seal? They decided in favor of the caribou.

The men gathered their bows, arrows, spears, and dry

food for each pack. They were dressed warmly in their two-layer hunting pants. The inner layer was made from a soft-furred animal, such as squirrel or rabbit, with the fur turned in next to the skin. The outer pants were made of either caribou or sealskin, with the hair turned away from the body.

Inerluk told his daughter to tell Kiachook where they were going, and that it would be either late today, late the next day, or at the most the day after when they returned, depending upon how good the hunting was. Nedercook wanted to go with them, but the tone of her father's voice when he said "No" was final.

After they had left and her mother was still away, she took her bow from the corner, put some arrows into her hunting sack, along with a piece of dry food, and headed out across the snow-covered tundra.

She would go out to the little creek where they got the ptarmigan. The bushes were now much shorter and there were big, hard drifts here and there. There were also some soft spots where the willows were dense, and made some shelter from wind. Here the snow was soft enough for tracks to be seen. As she walked she looked to right, and then to the left, then she scanned the snow for tracks of any kind, then her eyes took in the horizon and the sky. She continued walking, and looking until she noticed fresh duck tracks. The tracks were so unexpected it almost scared her, and she came to a stop. For one crazy moment the thought ran through her mind, Am I dreaming duck, a duck up here in the snow-filled creek? She knew that all but one kind of duck had long left the sea. All that were left were the big black ducks, and they had disappeared when the ice closed the water in front of the village. Her heart pounded faster. If only I can get it, she thought, before it gets limbered up, when it starts to walk again.

She carefully fitted an arrow to her bow and, holding it ready, started forward. She knew the partly-drifted tracks were made when the duck first landed. It had walked, but it would rest sooner or later because it would be tired from being blown inland from the open water. She hoped the long, cold rest would make it clumsy when it started moving again. She put her parka hood down so she could hear better, and so the duck would not see the ruff on the hood. Carefully she would peek over each high, drifted ridge — no duck. The tracks were lost in places where the snow was drifted harder.

At the third crest of hard snow, as she was inching her head to peek over, she saw the duck. It was still in a sitting position where it had probably rested since it found this sheltered spot. She almost trembled as she aimed her arrow. The bird had seen her, but because it was just the upper part of her hoodless head, it was not alarmed; however it was starting to raise itself.

Nedercook let the arrow fly and, unbelievable even to her, it hit its mark! In her excitement she tumbled into the deep snow, but she soon had the big duck in her hands. When she was sure it was dead she sat in the snow. She was so happy she whispered "Quiana" (thank you) to herself as she examined the big black bird. Then she put it into her hunting sack and picked up her bow from where it lay in the snow. She felt elated, happy, proud and thankful. She wanted to run home quickly, but then she remembered that everyone was away, so she decided to take her time. Still her excitement would not let her linger.

Her mother looked up inquiringly as she entered.

"Papa and them," she said, "went to Ignutak hunt for caribou, they be late, maybe tomorrow or more before come home."

Removing her packsack and holding it by the strap, she held it out to her mother.

"Heavy," her mother said as she put it down on the floor in front of her. Then she opened the pack and looked in.

"Duck?" with an unbelieving voice she continued, "Where?" as she pulled it from the packsack.

Nedercook needed no more to start her off on her story. When she had finished her mother reached over with one arm to her daughter, kneeling beside her, and held her close for a few moments. No words were needed. She felt loved as she looked at the duck her mother held in her other hand. She also felt proud in a humble sort of way, proud maybe that her mother loved her, and proud that she had contributed her bit to the food supply.

"Too good, we skin and save for parka," her mother said as, like a caress, she ran her hand across the feathers. That made Nedercook even happier, because she knew they had been saving the tougher skins of the diving ducks until there would be enough for her father's parka. Now she had helped to add to it. Kiachook watched as her daughter carefully cleaned and cut the duck. She removed the insides, saving the main parts as she had seen her mother do. She carefully cut off the very ends of the wing tips to use as a whisk broom.

Kiachook picked up her ulu and together they removed as much fat and grease as they could by pushing the ulu against the skin and away from them, following the direction of the feather stubs. Then the skin was spread out to dry on a log with the skin side up.

Kiachook noted the expression on her daughter's face as she looked at her greasy, bloody hands and said, "Daughter do not worry about what is on the outside of the body — that can be washed clean. It is the dirt or decay that one collects in the soul that one should be concerned about."

Then she passed Nedercook a pot of water for cleaning, and she asked, "Want to start the cooking fire?"

"Yes," Nedercook replied as she quickly cleaned her hands.

Her mother had kept a small bed of coals alive in the

stormy day room, so she did not have to go to the Big
Dance House as so many others did. She soon had a
fire going and eventually the pot boiled. Nedercook kept
hoping her father and brothers would return before
dinner.

But when night came she settled down to eat with her
mother and sister, who was visiting while her husband,
Kimik, was away caribou hunting. The duck was tender
and they all enjoyed it. Her sister smiled and said,
"Nedercook, you hunt like a man." This praise made
her feel proud.

"I'll tell you a story," Paniagon offered when bedtime
came.

> This will be the story of a little mouse who was
> running back and forth across a rotten skylight when
> suddenly it gave way beneath him. He fell down
> through the air until he hit a cross beam. He held on
> to it. Here he decided to spend the night.
>
> Next morning the mouse slipped and fell from the
> beam. He fell down as far as the benches or seats in the
> house, so he said, "I'll spend the night here."
>
> The next day he fell to the floor. He started to walk
> around the floor, but then he fell down the basement
> steps. He looked out and saw a big fire. He did not know
> what to do, but figured he was trapped in the building
> and the only way he might save himself was to dash
> out past the fire and risk getting scorched in doing so.
> When he was safely past the fire he looked back and
> saw that it was only a sunbeam.
>
> Then he thought, surely there must be something
> wrong with me to make a mistake like that. So I think
> I will go over there and fight those two big roots. He
> made his attack, and as he struggled he broke off pieces
> and finally he tore them both down. When he was
> through he was so exhausted that he fell asleep. When
> he woke up he discovered that what he thought were
> big roots or stumps were just two little pieces of rotten
> wood. Again he repeated "What is wrong with me?"
>
> He continued a little way until he came to a big lake.
> "I think I will cross this big lake," he said to himself,

"even if it is so wide that I cannot see the other side."
When he had crossed to the other shore he looked back
and then he saw that it was only a man's footprint filled
with water.

He repeated again, "What is wrong with me?" So he
looked around and said, "Well, I think I will cut down
the pole or post that holds up the sky. But first I will
dig a deep tunnel to run into when it falls, so I will not
be hurt!" Finally he finished the tunnel. He started to
chew on the pole or post that held up the sky. When
it started to fall he dashed into his tunnel and shivered
in fright as he heard a terrible noise and the ground
above him shook.

When everything was quiet and still, he very carefully
came out from the tunnel. Then he saw that what he
had cut down was just a big leaf.

Nedercook liked this story and told her sister so.

Next morning there was still no sign of the hunters.
Nedercook took some duck and soup to old Oopick.
She felt good as she saw the happy smile crease the
wrinkled face, and when Oopick said, "You good
hunter," Nedercook smiled her bashful smile.

Around noon Nutchuk and Kimik walked into the
inne. As they removed their heavy packsacks, Nutchuk
explained, "Come for sleds, we find plenty caribou.
Oolark and papa get two between them, Kimik get one,
I get one." They expressed surprise when Nedercook
gave them each a small piece of duck to go with their
meal. She saved a larger piece for her father.

With Komo's help the two men left, pulling the sleds.
The dog seemed eager to go out with his master, Kimik.

It was getting dark the following day when the hunters
topped the little rise, slowly approaching the inne,
pulling behind them sleds piled high with caribou. The
women rushed forward to greet them. There was much
happiness in their voices. The men looked tired, but they
stored the meat out of the reach of dogs, first bringing
one caribou carcass inside. Then they left to help Kimik.

The next stop would be the Big Dance House, where

they would clean their bodies before returning to eat. It was similar to a sauna but the villagers called it bathing, or taking a bath. Dinner was ready by their return. All ate, laughed, and talked. This was a happy occasion. Food was stored against the cold winter. Some of the meat would be given to other members of the village.

Next day the women would skin the caribou, saving the leg skins for mukluks. Kiachook was pleased to have some caribou brains to rub on the skins to soften them. They were not aware that this contributed to the odor of their garments and their dwellings. They had always smelled strong odors and were accustomed to them. Odor meant food and food meant life.

There was no lock on Inerluk's cache, but he did not worry because there were unwritten laws that the whole village abided by, rules made at the very beginning of this village. No one ever stole anything from another villager, be it food, personal belongings, or another man's wife. These rules of conduct were taught to children early in life.

When a wrong was committed the elders of the village met in the Big Dance House. They would elect three of the strongest men who, with their primitive weapons, went to the accused man. Then the four would go for a walk. If it was winter (as it so happened only once in the life of Nedercook while she lived in the village of Rocky Point) the men would go walking out of sight of the village, maybe to the open water if there was some. Later the three elected men would return. None of the villagers ever saw the violator again. With this law, each understood that to live was the greatest of privileges, and like innocent children they lived in harmony with the elements and with one another. Nedercook did without her usual story that evening so her tired father could rest.

The next day they spent caring for the caribou meat.

It was a happy day for the Inerluk family. Inerluk announced to his family after the evening meal, "Tomorrow we shall rest, each in our own way, do only little things." As he looked at his family and the drying sinew and meat, he continued, "On these days we should feel thankful in our hearts to the giver of all gifts." He looked about, much as Kiachook had when she seemed to be thanking the universe for good fortune. "Tomorrow we will let the land belong to itself," he smiled at his family as he continued. "This shall be our way of saying thank you, we are greatful to the provider that governs all the land."

Nedercook always liked these days because her family was not preoccupied or rushing off here and there after food. On these infrequent days that her father chose for the family to rest and build strength against coming struggles there was time for her to ask questions.

Kiachook extracted fat from caribou suet by heating it in a pot. She decided to make a big bowl of ice cream. She felt relaxed and happy. There was no rush, for this was a day to enjoy. As she sat there using her hand as a beater she began to sing a song that had much humming between the words:

Raven and Hawk Song

Once long ago a raven sat on a treetop and as he surveyed the surrounding area he saw a hawk.

The hawk was eating a freshly killed ptarmigan.

As the raven watched he thought how nice it would be if he, too, could be like the hawk and get his own fresh food.

But he was only a lowly scavenger.

Then he got an idea and he spoke to the hawk. "Hawk, hawk over there, I cannot eat the fresh food, raw meat, like you are doing."

But the hawk paid no attention to him and continued to eat.

When the hawk had finished eating, he turned to the raven and said, "Raven, raven over there, I do not want to eat the things that you eat, the garbage and the scavenging."

Then as he took off he flew past the raven with a big, graceful sweep as he rose into the sky. As soon as the hawk was out of sight the raven quickly flew over to the fresh ptarmigan remains and ate up all that the hawk had left.

When Kiachook finished the song she asked Nedercook to bring her a little clean snow and some berries. When Nedercook returned her mother started another song. There was also much humming in this song and between the words. It was called:

Man Without Mittens
Once there was a man
whose mittens were all worn out.
He had no material with which
to make new ones.
He did not like the idea
of getting up without mittens,
But he had to anyway.

Early in the day Nedercook had fetched some salty sea water to add to the cooking of the caribou. As the pots simmered, tantalizing aromas filled the inne. Paniagon and Kimik were invited to share this evening's meal of caribou, vegetables, greens and ice cream. This was an evening of rejoicing; laughter and talk filled the inne. It was on this evening that they learned that Paniagon was to have a baby sometime toward spring.

When the quiet of evening came, Nedercook lay in her bed thinking of the stories and legends she had learned. This was part of the education of all the village children, so the legends and stories would not change with the passing of time, nor would they be lost. She enjoyed learning and was good at memorizing. Each evening's story was a joy to her. She never considered it a task, as some of the young did. She said, "Papa, you are not tired tonight, tell me a long, long story."

92

After a brief silence, he said, "We have just eaten caribou, so I will tell you a legend of long ago."

Once there were two brothers. One had a wife and the other was unmarried. The married brother decided that his wife should accompany them on their fall caribou hunt. After traveling for many miles they decided to stop and build a hunting camp. The wife was to stay at the camp. She would prepare the food while the men hunted for caribou.

Before the brothers left her alone, they warned her very strongly against letting anyone touch or bother her head. As they started to leave her husband turned to her again and said, "Be very, very careful that no one touches your head."

When they were gone the wife felt very lonely. She was alone for two days. On the third day she saw a little woman coming to her camp. The wife was happy now she would have some company. The little woman seemed very friendly, so the hunter's wife did not worry. As they talked the little woman slowly edged closer to the hunter's wife, all the while carrying on a friendly conversation. When she was within touching distance of the hunter's wife, the little woman suddenly exclaimed, "Oh, what is that in your hair?"

As she said this, she reached out and touched the head of the unsuspecting hunter's wife. That was it, with the touch of the stranger's finger her brain seemed to go numb. The little woman hurriedly left.

When the two brothers returned they knew that something was wrong, because the wife could not even hear noises. They guessed what had happened.

Since they had brought home a freshly killed caribou's head, the brothers decided to transfer the brain of the caribou to the head of the woman. This they proceeded to do. When they were finished, she could hear again and things seemed all right until one day there appeared the start of horns on her head. Then her whole countenance began to change and her head took on the shape of a caribou's head. Next her whole body changed into that of a caribou.

The brothers wanted to get the rest of the meat and bring it to camp, but fearing other hunters might, without knowing, kill the wife, they decided to tie her up inside of the shelter while they were away. They returned that evening to find that she was gone. Somehow she had freed herself. They gave up everything else and began searching for the missing wife.

For days they searched long and hard, but they could not find her, so they finally returned to the village. The man married to the woman who had turned into a caribou asked the women of the village to make him lots of mukluks. Taking all of the mukluks in a pack, he left to search again for his wife.

One day he became very tired and drowsy so he decided to lie down and rest on top of a little knoll. First he put his hunting sack on the ground to use as a pillow. When his head touched the hunting sack he could hear someone talking. The voices seemed to come from inside the knoll.

"Grandma, tell me a story," pleaded the voice inside the knoll.

"I have no story to tell," came another voice.

The first voice now sounded on the verge of tears as it begged, "Grandma tell me a story."

"Very well," came the grandmother's voice, "I'll tell you a story."

She began;

"Once upon a time there were two brothers. One took his wife with them when they went hunting, but her brain was stolen and replaced by a caribou's. They tied her up but she escaped and, although they searched and searched for her, they could not find her. So they gave up and went back to the village. They did not know where to find her, but she is a black caribou and she lives with a herd of caribou over on the Siberian side.

After hearing this, and more, the man headed back to his village as fast as he could. There he ordered a big hunting packsack full of mukluks, an extra parka, and mittens.

Then he took off for Siberia. (During this time land bridged the two continents.)

When he reached the Siberian side there was an enormous herd of caribou. He searched for the black one that the mysterious voice beneath the knoll had spoken of.

94

After many, many days he finally spotted a black caribou. Then he carefully began to work his way closer and closer to it, sneaking behind the other caribou in this large herd.

Finally he grabbed the black caribou and as he did so he pulled his knife and slit the underside as the voice in the knoll had said he should. Carefully he finished the slit and before him fell his wife, just as she looked when they had first gone on the caribou hunt.

From his packsack he brought the parka, mukluks and mittens that he had carried with him, as the mysterious voice in the knoll had said he should if he was to bring his wife home safely. Both happily returned to their village.

This time it was Nedercook who was almost asleep by the time the story was finished, but she managed to mumble a sleepy, "Thank you," before rolling over to sleep.

The next day dawned clear and nice. Inerluk and his sons went on another caribou hunt, this time taking the sleds with them. They knew that other men were hunting, as word of their success had spread through the village. This time Nedercook did not ask to go.

CHAPTER 15
FESTIVAL TIME

T he days of winter were getting shorter and darker, but excitement was growing in the village, especially among the young unmarried women. They remembered how Kimik, one of the better hunters of the village, had fallen in love with Paniagon, who was now married to him and expecting. To the young women it all seemed to have happened at the festival. Nedercook knew differently, but she was not saying anything, preferring to remain quiet.

This year Nedercook was old enough to practice the "Women of the Sea" dance. If she learned it well enough for the elders to approve, she could star in it at the festival. She wanted to do this, and she wanted to do it well, because it was the most beautiful and the most graceful of all the dances and because she wanted to be one of the performers. So she practiced and practiced. This was always done during the middle part of the day, because by then all able-bodied men would have left the Big Dance House. Older women who knew the dances would come and do the dance the girls were learning. Then they could practice while the elders watched the beginners and advised if wrong motions were used. Nedercook loved doing the dance and, having one of the more slender, supple bodies, was able to perform it beautifully and with grace.

Inerluk and his sons returned late on the third day. They were pulling the sled. This time, because they had only one sled, they had packed it differently. They had skinned out the bodies, leaving the legs attached to the skin. They had placed the caribou hide hair side next to the sled and then filled it with the cut meat. They had filled the sled to overflowing, lashing the heads on top. One man worked the handlebars, mostly to keep the sled from tipping over. The two in front pulled. They would stop along the way to change places.

"You lucky," Kiachook called as the women rushed to meet them.

"We get three," Inerluk replied.

"We hungry." The voices seemed to come from both of the sons.

"We have cooked," stated Kiachook.

"Festival day is day after tomorrow," Nedercook said. She hopped happily about the sled as it continued to the inne.

Dinner was a happy but silent occasion. The men were busy satisfying their appetites, so they ate mostly in silence except for an occasional "Good."

The women understood because they all had been out on hunts of one kind or another during windy, cold days. They knew how it felt to be hungry and tired, and how nice the feeling was to finally get to shelter, warmth and food. Relating to this, they let their tongues be still.

When the men stopped in satisfaction, highlights of the hunt and news of the festival to come poured forth. The two brothers left to retire. Inerluk lay down and immediately fell asleep.

Whenever possible the villagers saved their urine. Kiachook had made a special, large clay pot for this. The uric acid in it was the only cleaning agent they had that could cut grease.

It was used occasionally as a liquid soap to remove excess grease and dirt from their hair, after which warm water was used to rinse away the smell and dirt.

Urine was also used to clean some skins that were very oily. It was in greater demand before the big festival, when looking one's best was of greater importance.

Dawn of the big day was calm and not too cold. Villagers bustled about. Those who had not already done so cut dried meat, fish, and food into bite-size pieces and put them in containers to take. Women were busy mixing ice cream. Kiachook had made hers while the men were hunting and had put it in a cold place to keep. Women with a little sewing left to do sewed faster. Those who were too poor to contribute anything else went tomcod fishing and, if they caught any, would bring them frozen. It was a custom also that the first food item a young hunter caught, be it meat or fish, was saved for this day. It was then presented and shared by the oldest of the village and by the parents and family. When Nedercook had killed her first snipe in the fall, Kiachook had cleaned and dried it whole so it could be properly presented.

Kiachook's two daughters helped her most of the day. Everyone was excited as the sun began to set. Soon now it would be time for everyone to go to the Big Dance House. Villagers and visitors came carrying their gifts of food, skins or other contributions. Each brought his own plate, and anyone who had a knife brought it also. After descending the steps to the long passageway, they left the food there or in a side room until serving time. The people climbed the steps at the other end of the passageway and entered through a large circular opening to the Big Dance House. Each carried his own packsack with him.

Performers placed their sacks by a relative; this way, when it came to gift-giving time each would know where his personal gifts were. These gifts were twisted sinew, mukluks, and any little thing that one wished to give to another.

The villagers sat in a large semi-circle, many deep, facing the circular opening in the floor through which they had entered, and through which the food and the performers would come. The soft glow from the seal oil lamps did not completely hide the keen expectation on their faces.

After all the villagers were seated, the first performers to come through the opening were men. They were dressed in long, fancy mukluks, short jacket-type parkas, and long, fancy gloves that came to the elbow and from which hung rattles (pieces of dried bone). They shook these to add accompaniment to the songs they would sing while dancing. They walked to the side reserved for the performers and stood facing the now-silent crowd.

"From our midst we will call forth two forecasters," said one of the performers as he motioned with his gloved hand. From the crowd one man and one woman stood up and came toward him. "You are the wise ones," said the man who had called them. As the two stood quietly before him, he continued speaking to the crowd, "This man will go out on the sea ice and this woman will go out on the tundra. When they return they will tell us what they have seen." Then his fancy-gloved hand made a motion toward the circular opening. The man and woman turned in silence, descended the steps, and disappeared.

Two male dancers came through the circular floor opening and the drummers began to beat upon their drums. The drummers were seated upon the floor opposite the villagers, chanting accompaniment as their bodies swayed forward, to the right, to the left, and back to their original position. Their bodies kept rhythm to the beating of the drums.

The two men started to dance, then each picked up a dry stalk of the wild plant the villagers called the *eeg-gee-took*. Each man placed his stalk against the wall. This dance showed, in motion and song, how the wild plant grew, where it grew, its uses, and of its tall, hollow stalks, and then showed in motion how high it grew. It described the dry clusters on top where many small flowers had bloomed in summer, but now were only a dry, dead-grass color. It showed the care taken by those who had gathered them so the tops had not broken off. This was all told in song and in mock picking motions, as if gathering imaginary plants and bringing them to the Big Dance House where they were to give peace, joy and a reminder of warmer days to all who looked upon the dry plant. The dancers then went to stand behind the two men with fancy gloves.

With the ending of the dance there emerged a group carrying the dry plant with the long stalks. These people were called the capable ones. A dozen or so of the best and biggest stalks were chosen from this bunch and laced loosely together with thin rawhide, in such a way that they would stand together in a natural position. This was then placed in the center of the room. The remaining stalks were tied, two together to form an X, and placed next to the wall at various points around the room. Everyone watched these capable ones at work. After the last decoration was placed, there followed two drum beats and then silence as two women quietly came up the entrance way, each carrying a large plate. In the center of the plates were balls of berries about the size of a lemon. The berries were held together with a fluffy binder. This was passed around to each person. As soon as the two women had descended the stairs and were out of sight, drums and chanting began again.

The two men dancers sang and pantomimed through another song. This song told of seal hunters going out on the sea ice to hunt, and of those lucky enough to get seals. It described saving, inflating and drying the bladder, and on this note the song stopped.

Next the loud-voiced announcer gave the name of the hunter and the number of seals he had taken during the year. One of the capable ones would emerge from the circular opening carrying the hunter's inflated seal bladders and would hold them high, as a hearty yell came from the audience. Some carried at least a dozen while others only one. The capable ones then hung the bladders from the ceiling.

The drums began again and this time the song was a happy one, of a hunter proudly bringing to his parents his first contribution. When the song was over, it was announced that it was time to give the young hunters credit. Dishes with the first catch of a species of either bird, animal or fish by a child were handed up to one of the capable ones, who stood near the top of the steps, out of sight of the audience. He took the dish that was handed to him and then he gently pushed it up so it appeared to slide up by itself out of the entrance way and onto the floor of the Big Dance House. The announcer called out the name of the item, and the name of the hunter.

Nedercook's heart beat faster when she saw the first snipe she had brought home. Her mother had saved it by drying it, and now she had it perched on top of a heaping bowl of Eskimo ice cream. She listened like the others to the description. When her name was mentioned, the great yell that followed was to ring in her mind for over one hundred years, whenever she recalled this event.

When all of the young hunters' dishes were on the floor, relatives went forth to carry them to some older person they wished to share with; afterwards it was taken to the hunter's family.

Paniagon picked up Nedercook's bowl and carried it to Oopick, who took a small piece of the snipe and some of the ice cream before it was carried to Nedercook's parents. After they had taken what they wanted, the large bowl of ice cream was passed around until it was gone. While this was going on, other dishes of food were slid onto the floor and the capable ones helped the young women, who would be dancing, to carry the big dishes around to all the villagers. The plates overflowed with food as everyone talked, ate and laughed. Dishes of berries, leaves in oil, and other dishes, some that needed a ladle, were also passed around. Foods such as meat, dried fish, Eskimo potatoes, and all other goodies that did not need ladles were passed and each picked off some to put on his plate. At this celebration you could eat all you wanted, and what you could not eat on your plate you took home; everyone always brought his biggest plate.

Nedercook did not have to help with the serving because she was one of the young hunters who were honored this evening. Sitting in a row with some of the others, she watched her sister. Paniagon was wearing the fancy new parka that had taken so much of her time before the festival. She seemed to glide about the large room. Her cheeks were rosy. Nedercook figured that her sister must have done what young women often did before entering the Big Dance House. They pinch their cheeks. Nedercook had never done it, but this evening as she watched the soft light from the many seal oil lamps which fluttered dimly, gently, and then more brightly upon her sister as she moved near, she had never seen her sister look more beautiful. While watching she had second thoughts about sewing and the pinching of one's cheeks. She also noted the look of tenderness on Kimik's face whenever Paniagon would stop before him with a tray of food.

As the food was served, the two plates of the forecasters, who had not yet returned, were never passed by. Something was always added to their plates by the capable ones. About two hours had passed since the forecasters had left. While the food was still being passed around, they appeared at the entrance way. Silence fell over the room. All the capable ones and servers stopped where they were, setting down the trays they were carrying and then seating themselves on the floor. The forecasters walked in silence to the performer's side and sat down by their plates. After finishing two mouthfuls of food, the male forecaster stood up and faced the villagers.

"See plenty seals," he said. Like a wave, the sigh of relief could be heard passing through the crowd, followed by yells of joy from the men. Silence returned as he seated himself.

The female forecaster then ate two mouthfuls of food. She stood, walked to the place where the other forecaster had stood, and faced the crowd. "See many berries," she declared. "Quana, quana" (thank you, thank you), the joyous chorus of women voices filled the big room. Joy was expressed because, if forecasters "see lots of berries and seals," it will mean good times; food would be plentiful for another year. If, on the other hand, they return and "see" nothing, as sometimes they do, then the people of Rocky Point would expect hard times for the coming year. Hard times meant lack of food, hunger, and often death for some of the villagers. The forecaster then returned to her seat and the two began a belated dinner.

As if by silent signal, the servers rose to resume the serving of food. This continued for a few hours. The people of the village were happy, a good year was forecast and, for a moment, they were secure, warm, and surrounded by family and friends. Food was abundant this evening and gifts would soon be next; each member had in different ways contributed to this evening's pleasure, so all felt the joy of giving.

The Rocky Point Eskimos were not a tribe of nervous, worried people. They knew what it was like to be cold, hungry, tired, and to go without when there was nothing. They knew death and hard times, but they did not make a day miserable by dreading, worrying, and complaining when times were hard. They tried to utilize all game to the fullest and to put away as much as they could against future hunger. The general outlook was that tomorrow would be better, which made it easier to enjoy the present.

A dozen or so women stood up and took their places in the half-circle around the entrance way. The drums began to beat and the drummers began to chant. The women began their dances. One moved a few steps in front of the double row of dancers. She was the star of this dance, and her every move was followed in smooth repetition by those behind her as she went through the motions of the seal skinning dance. With graceful movements she gave the imaginary seal a drink of fresh water. Then with an imaginary ulu she removed the head, all the while keeping her rhythmic movements coinciding with the beat of the drums. Next she removed the skin, then fleshed off the blubber, cut it into pieces that fit into a seal poke, and fastened the opening. She then carried the head back to the sea. All the time her body swayed in unison with the drum beats. With the returning of the seal's head to the salty water, the drum beats were faster, then the dance was over.

The dancer quickly stepped back to make room for the next dancer. A very young woman came forward. She looked small as she stood to do the berry picking dance. Her eyes rested on no one as she conveyed the impression of scanning the hillsides to decide where to go. Making up her mind, she went through the motions of starting out. The drums speeded a little. Then as she picked the imaginary berries, the drums speeded considerably; she was picking. The dancers behind her followed her movements. Next she was returning with the heavily loaded seal poke. Here the drums slowed as if they, too, were struggling, slow, tired. Finally, a happier note came as she had an imaginary bowl of berries. Silence again, the dance was over.

Paniagon came forward. She was to do the sewing dance. On the third drum beat Paniagon's body began to move, trudging imaginary miles to snare the ground squirrel, skin and dry it (a woman's parka usually took 30 skins, a man's 40), and returning to tan the skins. As Paniagon stood in front of all the villagers, the lamplight caught and reflected a little shine here and there as it fell upon her fancy new squirrel parka. The many wolverine tassels, some having an inch of wolf fur on the end, danced about as her body swayed and her arms swept to the right or the left in circular motions. It was a beautiful sight to watch her go through the motions of cutting the many skins, and see the large, graceful sweep of her right hand and arm as she began sewing the parka. As her two hands went forward with palms open, pausing momentarily away from her, the audience knew that another task was started. She then went through the motions of twisting sinew.

Kiachook, sitting on the floor, watched her daughter, all the while her head and upper body moving in rhythm with the beat of the drums. Pride and joy were reflected in her old face, just as they would when Nedercook danced the Women of the Sea dance. Again silence filled the room. Paniagon stepped back.

"Boom, boom, boom," began the drums, and Nedercook knew it was the signal to start the beautiful Woman of the Sea dance. In this dance she started alone, with no backup dancers. Her lithe body could move with much ease. This showed in all of her graceful movements. She was a Woman of the Sea out on a fishing trip. Gliding about, she pretended to be searching for fish. Her hair, usually worn in long braids, was hanging loose so it fell in long, dark strands from her young head, over the parka, to her waist.

As if seeing a fish, Nedercook disappeared into the circular opening for a moment or two, and then surfaced with an imaginary fish held in her little brown hands. She proceeded to eat it daintily, all the while swimming about in the imaginary sea water. She circled around the opening again as if looking for another fish, then, as if seeing one, disappeared from sight. As she did this, the drums and chanting speeded up and the volume increased, stopping on one last wild "boom." The dance was over. Silence filled the room until Nedercook stepped shyly up from the circular opening to be greeted with wild, happy shouts of approval.

Married women began passing out balls of frozen berries, which were held together with a fluffy binder of oil mixed with other ingredients. They were a little smaller than a popcorn ball. This was refreshing, for the room was hot and stuffy. Many villagers had removed their outer parkas and folded them as pillows to sit on. For fresh air the skylight had been opened at the beginning, but this did little good.

Again the drums began. This time the men did the dancing, mostly hunting dances, like stalking and killing the caribou, harpooning the seal or whales, and always the triumphant return. After several dances by the men the drums stopped and the women who had danced earlier joined the men. When the drums started it was a happy combination dance.

When this was over it was gift-giving time. Many of the gifts were small exchanges, but they were appreciated as much as the larger ones. Much emphasis was put on the fact that one *remembered*. Even if it was a very small gift, the receiver was happy because he was not forgotten. This always brought happiness to the giver.

A few of the well-to-do men (they were the better hunters) would go down to the first passageway where they had left large bundles containing skins, sinew and furs. Carrying these up through the circular opening, they would sit down and cut off pieces of skin large enough for a pair of mukluk soles. This would continue until the skin was gone. From the sealskin the giver would cut long, narrow pieces for a new belt or bands to go around mukluks. They began with the most needy, who would receive the better gifts.

Typical gifts passed out, beside the skin and furs, would be twisted sinew, ulus, mukluks, rugs, baskets and storage containers for vegetables. Needles were so hard to come by that they were rarely given, but rather saved for barter or trade.

After all the gifts and food were passed out, all the men connected with a successful black whale hunting party during the past year would join what they called the lucky ones. They gathered at the open skylight outdoors and sang a certain victory song called the Successful Whale Hunters Song.

This always thrilled Nedercook as she sat with all the others in the dimly lit room. Everyone was looking toward the skylight from which the song came loud and clear. The shadowy silhouette of a head could be seen every once in a while as one of the men next to the skylight, those who had actually harpooned the whale, would put his face down near the opening. They were the men of the inner circle; the men of the outer circle were standing. They were the ones who had helped in the hunt. Every man sang, all singing this song in a loud, happy voice of victory. There was silence when the song was over, but not for long.

The beat of drums brought all the dancers, who had quietly slipped to the lower level, and the singers of the whale song emerging from the entrance way, all waving high above their heads long white ribbons of dried seal intestines. This was an exuberant, happy entrance. The drums beat loud and wild. Then all the women who could get to their feet stood up and joined in dancing.

While the last of the dances was taking place, several men left the celebration and went down to the sea to cut a large hole in the ice about a thousand feet from shore, five to six feet square. The capable ones had collected the seal bladders and returned them to the hunters who had contributed them for decorations. All came to watch the hunters sink the now deflated bladders into the hole, along with some sausage-like links of seal intestines filled with choice foods. This was the finale of the big festival; with the sinking of the last bladder, all the young people raced back to the big room in the Dance House, while others trudged wearily back up the hillside. Then the young assisted anyone who needed help carrying gifts home.

This celebration was an annual affair, which began on one evening and always lasted until the next morning's light. In the past, it had been known to have lasted for three days and nights. It all depended upon the number of people in the village, the number of visitors, and the amount of food and gifts to be given away.

CHAPTER 16
MARRIAGE

Activity around the village was quiet for the next couple of days. For Nedercook it soon returned to normal. She remembered that last year had been different because, while the resting and recovery were taking place, Kimik had convinced Paniagon that she should become his wife. Nedercook was not sure how, but Kimik, Paniagon and her parents had all agreed to this — and without Nedercook's opinion. Within a week her sister was publicly declared Kimik's wife at the Big Dance House before the elders of the village. Then she moved out of her childhood home.

Nedercook missed her sister, but she knew that this had to be. In the future, if and when one of her brothers took a wife, he could bring her to their old home. But if no room was left because of other brothers or sisters, and the wife's place was not crowded, they could go there. This was done as often as the first. If both places were full, then the men of both families and friends from the village gave of their time to help dig and make a new home.

Nedercook decided that it was not as if her sister had married a stranger from another village and moved away, so she accepted, like others of her family, that Paniagon had made a good choice. "I shall learn more of the stories and legends than anyone else." Nedercook decided, "and then I shall not miss my sister." So this evening as things were more or less back to normal after the big festival, she said, "Tell me a story, a long story, Papa."

He was silent for awhile and then he said, "This will be about a young woman."

Long ago there was a young woman who lived at her parents' home. This daughter lived in one of the little side rooms off of the lower entrance way. Her parents lived on the floor above her. Every nice summer day she would go berry picking. When she returned she would give some of the berries to her parents, then she would descend to her room. Her parents would hear her giggling. Her laughter would rise and fall as if she had company and was sharing the berries with someone. Each time the daughter returned from a berry-picking trip the same sounds of giggling and laughter would rise and fall, always coming faintly from the daughter's room.

After a time the father became suspicious. Finally he could not stand it any longer, so the next time his daughter left to go berry picking he decided to investigate. He descended to her room and there at her bed was a human skull. Around the mouth was the stain of berries. Her father in a horrified stupor picked up the skull and carried it to the highest part of the cliff, and with a big heave tossed it over the edge.

In the evening when their daughter came home, she made her usual stop first at her parents, giving them some berries as she had done countless times before. Then she happily left for her room. Soon the parents heard instead of the usual giggles and laughter, a very, very sad sobbing. After a time the father could not stand to hear the sadness. He descended to the lower room. He called when he got to the skins that hung by her door, and asked what was wrong. When he entered she looked at him through tear-stained eyes and said broken-heartedly, "My thing — it is gone." She had the saddest look a father had ever seen.

He could not bear to look at her and not speak, so he heard himself say, "If it was the skull, I took it and threw it away."

Like a person in a trance, she arose and went out through the door. He saw that she took the very same steps he had taken when he carried the skull to the cliff's edge, then she pulled the parka hood to cover her face. Before he could move or cry out, she jumped over the cliff's edge.

She felt herself falling and falling until there was a sudden stop. Some time after this she saw some fish, but as she got closer to them she realized that they were people. As she came closer she saw that they were very clean people. Never before had she seen or smelled anyone who was as clean as these people.

She asked them if a man had passed this way before she came. "Yes," they said, "a short time ago. He went that way," indicating with a sweep of their hand.

She traveled on in this direction until she saw some large-mouthed fish, rock fish, she thought, but as she approached, they too turned into people. She decided to ask them about a certain man. "Oh, yes," they said as they pointed in the same direction as the clean people had. They saw him go that way a short time ago. She went on and finally she came to a large meeting house. People of her village called this kind of big house the Big Dance House. It also served for all meetings.

She looked into the big room and there was her man, and in his arms he was holding another woman. Somehow he was aware that she had followed him. Looking at her, he said, "Go home girl. You do not belong here — yet." Then, as she continued to stand there, he said, "Go home now, while you still can get there. Remember there are two roads and to make it home again you will have to take the rough one, don't, don't follow the easy, smooth path or you will never find your home. Go girl, go now, before it is too late."

She was hurt and angry, but she knew this was no place for her to stay alone, so she turned and saw the two paths. One looked so nice and easy, but he had said to be sure to take the rough one if she wanted to see her home again. So she started along the rough road, and it was rough with big rocks and dips. She continued struggling over the rough terrain for some time. Then she thought why should I struggle and fight this rough road when there is that nice, easy one over there just a little ways away?

So she stopped climbing over the rough rocky road. She left it for the easy, smooth one. It was very easy

111

going, with a little breeze blowing. She traveled swiftly, happy that she had made the change to an easier path. As she traveled this easy trail she looked away and saw that she had left the earth. It was down there below her. But now she could not stop herself and she went on as if drawn by some strong, invisible force.

She came to a door where two polar bears seemed to watch over a very old woman. The old woman had two large blades of bone with which she regulated the moon's light. The girl remembered that her home village always celebrated on the first evening of a new moon by shouting and howling happily to the new moon. Then she remembered that today was the day of the new moon, for the old lady was holding the bone so only a thin crack of light shone through.

The girl looked down at the earth below, and there she could see the joyous faces turned to the new moon as they danced about in joy, everyone happy for another new moon. This made the girl very homesick and she begged the old woman to tell her how she could return to her village. At first the old woman was not about to tell, but she pleaded so much that the old woman said, "All right, there is only one way left for you now, if you ever want to get back there. First you must sew up two kinds of mittens, one from caribou and the other from seal skin. When you have several pairs of mittens, follow this rope to the end. It is strong but it stops before it touches the earth. When you reach the end you will have to be brave and let go — just jump down — do not be scared, because if you are scared to jump and do not let go of the rope you will never get home again!"

After making many mittens the girl bravely descended, using mitten after mitten as she followed the rope. When she came to the end of the rope she saw the earth spread out below her, but she would have to drop some distance. As she hesitated and looked she became scared, the longer she looked the more afraid she became, until she could not let go of the rope. She clung to it in fear. She never returned home because she could not bring herself to let go of the rope.

Inerluk paused when he had finished, and then he said that a woman called Aut-ma-gook and some other man claimed they once saw what looked like a large human spider dangling in the sky, at the end of a rope that went up and up until the end was lost in space.

CHAPTER 17

UNDER-ICE NET

G oing to set seal net," Inerluk said the next day. Nedercook wanted to go along. She helped by carrying the chisel and the ice scoop to the sled. Her father put the bulky net, pole markers and anchors on the sled. Nedercook ran down the hillside while her father held on to the handlebars, keeping the sled from going too fast. When they reached the ice Nedercook helped by pulling on the rope that was fastened to the front, while her father pushed and tried to keep it from turning over on the rough trail. They followed along the shore for a ways.

After going from shore about two hundred feet, her father said, "We make hole here."

He circled the spot and Nedercook started energetically to chip away the ice with the primitive chisel. Her father walked on for another 65 feet or so and, selecting the right place, made another circle on the ice and snow. He walked back to his daughter and said, "I do this, you get pole."

She gladly gave him the chisel and walked quickly back over the trail. From behind the cache she took the long pole. The splices were wrapped with rawhide, securely joining the thin, long pole. Her father had always handled the pole with care. This was the first time he had trusted her to get the pole. She would be very careful, although he had not told her to do so. He just knew she would. Grabbing it near the front with her mittened hand, she dragged it out slowly over the ice. She remembered from other times how her father would chisel two large holes some distance apart. Then he would fasten the end of the long coil of rawhide rope to the end of the pole she was dragging. She would wait at the other hole while her father pushed the pole into the first hole, aiming the end for the hole where she was. How long it seemed before she could see either pole or the shorter piece of rawhide with the smooth wooden float attached! How eagerly she would hook whichever came closer to the hole! Because, to set the net, the rawhide rope had first to be pulled between the two holes. Then it was easy for her father to pull the net into the water, so the net was set between the two holes, with a strong piece of rawhide attached to each end.

Her father was almost down to water. The chisel had a strap secured to the handle; it was slipped over his parka-clad arm to prevent loss of the chisel. He had cut a circular hole almost down to water; then he left the center part and tried to chip evenly around the outer edge because he knew that, once he punctured through the ice, the salt water would come gushing up to fill the hole. When that happened he would not be able to see where the chisel point struck. He must chisel by feel, pushing the chisel down in the water and slush, and chipping where he felt an obstruction.

A last support was loosened and the center ice came bobbing up to the surface. When it was removed, Inerluk took the chisel and went to start the next hole, while Nedercook used the ice dipper to scoop away all the little pieces of ice. Finally, the hole was cleared of ice and Nedercook lay on her stomach and peered down into the icy water.

Picking up the ice dipper, she moved to where her father was working. "Let me do some," she said. Her father handed her the chisel. He walked back to the sled and removed the seal net. It was a big, bulky thing made from thinly cut rawhide (a real task when one considers that it was cut with their primitive tools). He placed the

115

notched end of the pole into the end of a coiled length of rawhide where there was a little loop, to which was fastened another short length of rawhide. The short piece of rawhide was attached to a short, smooth piece of very light wood; the float would help the other person to see and catch the rawhide. Carefully he lined up the pole so it pointed in the direction of Nedercook and the hole she was working on.

Then Inerluk went to his daughter and finished opening the second hole. When it was clear of ice, Nedercook lay down so her face hung over the edge of the hole as she tried to see bottom.

"Be careful," her father warned, because she could easily slip and fall into this large hole. A chill wind started to blow, so Nedercook pulled her parka hood up to protect her head. This was a work parka, so it had only a narrow band of wolverine around the face.

"See fish," she called, still on her stomach.

Her father came and peered into the water. "Tomcod," he said, "We set net, then maybe fish — if not too late."

Nedercook had accompanied her father on enough seal-net setting trips to know what to do and expect. So she waited by the last hole while her father walked back to the long pole. He placed the notched end in the center of the ice hole, and double-checked to make sure it was in line with the second hole. Slowly he eased the long, thin, flexible pole into the water under the ice. As he pushed he kept the tension on the rawhide line and let it slip slowly through his hands. Nedercook waited patiently. This was something that could not be hurried.

"You look hard," her father called when he figured the pole should be at her hole.

Nedercook lay on the ice again and stared and stared into the dark water. In her right hand she held a short pole with a hook attached at the end. She put her hands on each side of her face to help shade the light reflections, while keeping her grip on the hooking pole. It seemed like a long time, but it was less than fifteen minutes.

"See it, see it." she cried excitedly.

"Careful," Inerluk cautioned as he stopped pushing. Nedercook pushed the hook end of her short pole into the water, and after some misses she hooked the pole and pulled it from the side. Then she moved her hook a little and tried to hook the rawhide. She caught the length with the float and it surfaced; quickly she grabbed it as she lightly tossed aside the pole.

"Got it, got it," she shouted, as she held tightly onto the rawhide. Inerluk gave a quick pull back on the pole and Nedercook felt the rawhide free itself. She started pulling it to the surface and quickly tied it to one of the poles her father had marked for this. Then they readied the net so it would go into the hole without tangling, floats on one side, sinkers on the other. "You watch," he said, as he started for the second hole. She was responsible for keeping the net untangled and in the right position as it entered the water.

"Now!" called her father as he started to pull the net into the water. Nedercook guided it as best she could. Her father pulled slowly to make it easier for her. When all the net was in the water he continued to pull until he figured it was centered evenly between the two holes. Then he called, "Hold it," quickly fastened his end of the rope, and hurried across the ice to fasten the piece Nedercook held. The net was between 50 to 60 feet long, with a piece of strong rawhide running its entire length. He checked the tension at both holes and straightened up, saying, "It's all right."

They had worked so long that the daylight was nearly gone. Looking around, he said with a smile, "We work fast." He secured the ends of the ropes and they put up the pole markers. "Too late to fish," he said. Slowly they started home, he dragging the pole and Nedercook pushing the sled.

117

Oolark had hunted the wolf but had returned without a catch. Nutchuk had been luckier; he had a large tundra hare. Her mother was away when they returned, but she arrived soon after. She had walked over to Paniagon and Kimik's for a short visit and she had eaten with them. "Very good soup," was her description.

"Carefully skin rabbit," Kiachook said to Nedercook as she handed her the big ulu. It was customary for the young to learn as much as possible; parents and elders were always willing to help. Nedercook had seen her mother and sister skin many rabbits, and now she was the one who was going to do it. She laid the skinning

118

leather on the floor and placed the big rabbit on it. She would do as well as anyone. Once she started, it was not hard. She was careful not to cut holes in the skin. Then she set the skin aside while she cut the meat into cooking pot size. She wiped her hands on some dry grass, straightened out the skin, and hung it to dry, being careful to expose all parts to the air.

That evening the Inerluk family retired early. Since Nedercook had participated in the physical work she thought her father would be tired also.

Inerluk, although he was old in years, was still a strong, healthy man. His body knew only the abuse of hard work and sometimes food did not come "on time," as we know it. Since childhood his body had known only highly nutritional foods. Inerluk and his villagers were governed by feelings of the true self which did not depend upon artificial stimulants. Food, warmth and companionship were the desires of Nedercook's time.

Inerluk could tell that his daughter was tired, so he said, "We worked hard, I'll sing short song." He began to hum in the darkness, add a few words, then hum some more. It was called the

Child's Tomcod Song

A little boy at Rocky Point
used to go down to the ice cracks
in early spring to spear the tomcod
because he did not have a hook.

While he was doing this
he thought he heard a little voice singing,
"Little boy, spear me
and take me home to your mother
and she will cook me
and after you have all eaten
finish dinner with some
of the sour leaves . . . cooked.
This will be very good."

119

When the song was over the only sound coming from Nedercook's direction was of slow, steady breathing. He smiled. In the darkness Kiachook snuggled close to her husband and said, "It is lucky we have daughter." Inerluk held her close.

After a good breakfast Inerluk was going to check his nets, then fish for tomcod.

Nedercook wanted to go as she always did when there might be excitement ahead. This morning her mother had said that she could go with her father to check his net because her mother's big toe had hurt. (She called it hurt when there was a little jabbing or tingling sensation — no pain — in her big toe.) This would mean that something unusual or unexpected was about to happen, but nothing bad. When the sensation was a dull pain, something not so good would happen. Today's was a sensation of the unexpected.

Inerluk took his spear, the pulling rope, and the knife he always carried when he left the inne. Nedercook carried a hunting sack, fishing equipment, ice scoop and chisel. The wind from the day before had died down, but they knew that some of the snow would be blown into the holes. From a distance they spotted the two upright markers. It was a precautionary measure taken because coastal weather was too unpredictable. Wind, either gentle or strong, was the general rule, but a blizzard might also develop. Snow could cover the holes, leaving no evidence, and much time would be lost looking for them. There was also the danger of an unsuspecting hunter walking on a thinly-covered hole.

As Inerluk and his daughter drew nearer they could tell that the two poles nearer the holes had been moved. Nedercook felt excitement flow through her as they rushed forward. She threw off the light pack as they reached the first hole. Inerluk chopped a small circle around the rawhide rope. He was careful not to cut it. At the second hole he chiseled out the entire hole and

120

quickly cleared away the floating ice. Exciting as these moments are, Nedercook knew enough not to grab the line of rawhide. She stood tense as her father felt the line. His voice carried excitement as he said, "We got something. Untie the first part of other rope." Running, she quickly undid it. Rushing back to her father's side, she watched as he pulled in the rawhide and saw the net begin to come through the hole. Nedercook helped pull because, if the seal was not too tangled, it might become free before her father could spear it. If it was fresh-caught, it could have a little kick to it and struggle free as it was being pulled onto the ice.

"I see it," Nedercook said as the tail end of a seal started to come through the ice hole. Inerluk put down his spear quickly and with his bare hands grabbed the tail. They pulled the seal onto the ice.

"Good one." Inerluk sounded pleased. They untangled it from the net and pulled it a short distance from the hole, taking no chance of it slipping back in. Nedercook started to pull the rest of the net out of the water. It had to be straightened before resetting. "Papa, papa," she cried excitedly.

Quickly he grabbed the net in front of her and began pulling. He exclaimed in Eskimo, "Ar-nick-ka." Then added, "Something else."

Pulling a little more, he said, "It is moving." Nedercook seemed to hold her breath. Her heart pounded. Her father grabbed for his spear, never missing a pull as he did so. Before she expected it, a large oogruk's head was in the hole. Her father let the spear fly. She had never seen him move so fast.

"Pull!" he cried. They pulled. It was so big that it was a tight fit to get it through the hole. "Ar-nick-ka," he exclaimed in amazement.

They pulled the second mammal a little farther away from the hole before they untangled it from the net, then they pulled it still farther. Inerluk had never caught two at the same time before; nor did he in the future. Nedercook jumped about in joy. "We got two, we got two!" she exclaimed happily.

Quickly they straightened out the net before it froze. Inerluk went to the first hole to pull, while Nedercook slowly fed the net back into the water. After tying the ropes again, they went to look at the catch with eyes that shone with happiness. Here were food, meat, oil and skins. This was a wonderful gift from the deep waters. Nedercook knew this was special. There were many days in which her father would catch nothing.

Taking the bigger and more difficult thing first was

the usual way of doing things in Inerluk's family. The reasoning was that it is best to use the first burst of strength on the big task, and then the smaller task would not seem so hard. They carried one pull rope; two had never been needed. Inerluk tied the rope so the animal could be dragged head first. In this way there was no friction, as it was with the grain of the hairs.

"We leave pack," her father said. It was a slow pull home. The oogruk was very heavy and the trail rough. By both working, they made it across the ice. As they neared the beach, villagers saw the slow-moving pair and came to help pull their catch to the inne. While Inerluk untied it Nedercook dashed down the steps of the entrance way, through the passageway, and burst upon her startled mother, who looked up from stirring a pot of boiling rabbit.

"We got two," Nedercook exclaimed, "We got two!"

"Chuna?" (what) Kiachook questioned.

"Seal and oogruk," Nedercook said breathlessly. "Papa out there," she continued as she waved her hand toward the entrance way.

"Two, ar-nick-ka," her mother said unbelieving. Quickly she slipped her outer parka on and automatically pulled the cooking pot away from the fire as she started out with Nedercook close behind her.

"Quana, quana," (thank you, thank you) Kiachook said as she looked at the oogruk.

"We will go back for the seal," Inerluk said.

"Good," Kiachook's voice was happy.

As Nedercook and her father walked back their steps seemed light; for a time hunger would not be a worry. When they reached the net, Inerluk felt of the line and shook his head. It was empty.

After tying the pull rope to the seal, they shouldered their packs. Fishing was out for today. Then both checked lines and markers. They began the second pull homeward, struggling to get the seal over the rough ice.

This time they both felt a little tired. Slowly they pulled. The smaller animal felt as heavy to Nedercook as the bigger one. The pull up the hill was hard but, seeing some of the villagers watching, she pulled with renewed strength.

Kiachook was well along with the skinning. Eagerly Nedercook untied and coiled the pull rope while her father helped her mother by hanging meat and putting some in the cache. Kiachook gave her daughter a big pot. "Take Oopick some," she said. Kiachook had put in a variety of parts. Nedercook went hurrying off. Oopick's inne was always a happy place to go; she praised Nedercook and made her feel important in a nice way.

Oopick was sitting by her glowing coals. She had a woman's cup between her hands (cups without handles were called women's cups). She was sipping wild Hudson's Bay tea.

At dusk Nutchuk and Oolark came from the village. They had hunted without luck and were surprised and happy over their father's catch.

"Too dark," they said to their mother. "Skin it tomorrow." They carried the seal to the underground passageway. "We come in morning," they said, and their mother knew they would carry the seal outdoors.

"Rabbit cooked," Kiachook said as they entered and took their places. Each person cared for his own bowl, plate and knife. In summer they were wiped with a handful of grass; during the winter they were usually given the last cleaning with the forefinger, which was sucked off.

Before eating the rabbit Kiachook took a very small piece of the meat and put it in the fire. With thumb and forefinger she picked up a pinch of ashes, then holding it before her lips blew it away; this was supposed to release the animal's spirit. The rabbit was then eaten with green leaves and roots, and berries at the end of the meal.

125

Kiachook held up a shoulder-blade bone of the rabbit. It was relatively clear. "Born on clear day," she remarked. Had it been a cloudy shoulder-blade bone, she would have said it was born on a cloudy day.

"Tomorrow you take Paniagon some meat," Kiachook said.

"Eh-eh," (yes) her daughter said with a smile. She thought of the fun she would have telling her sister her version of today's good fortune. There was no story that evening. Everyone was tired and fell quickly to sleep.

CHAPTER 18

NEDERCOOK HURT

The cold, dark days of winter passed quickly for Nedercook. Now the days, although cold, were getting longer; the daylight hours came earlier and darkness, later.

On one clear morning Inerluk and Oolark were to go out to try for crabs. Nedercook had some skins to rub dry, so she would stay home. Her mother surprised her by looking up from her work and saying, "You go, I put skins in cold place. You come when sun is highest, soften them then."

The joy of going out made Nedercook step quickly. Taking the big mesh sack, she placed it on the sled where the men already had the other gear. The three traveled up the shoreline and then stopped before going out onto the ice. Inerluk studied the sky and weather carefully. "We try," he said. His concern before leaving the shore was well founded because, if one was careless and did not study the weather, he might walk out onto the ice of the Bering Sea and, unaware, be quietly taken on a ride to his death. Along the coast of Norton Sound from Nome, down past Rocky Point, the ice would often break loose quietly, sometimes in sections of many miles and at other times, in small pieces like a V or a U. It would break free one hundred to a thousand feet from shore and quietly leave, drifting to sea; at other times, it would break free several miles from shore. Very, very few men who have been taken out with the ice would ever make it back to the mainland. Due to its quiet departure, the gap was not noticed until a dark line could be seen from where the person stood. By then it was too wide to cross, usually about a quarter- to a half-mile of open water. The north wind then strikes suddenly, blowing in a wild fury and causing whitecaps going away from the shore. The water becomes rough, throwing spray on to the floating ice, then the movement breaks off sections so the piece becomes smaller and smaller as it drifts out to sea.

As Nedercook walked over the rough ice she looked at her father and Oolark and noticed that Oolark was built much like their father. He was not very tall, but stocky. Nutchuk took more after their mother. He was tall in build and stood at least a head taller than her father.

Even with the sled, the three walked quite fast. Oolark chiseled the new thin ice from the holes that he and his father had made the day before. Nedercook, using the willow strainer, bailed the slush out of the hole. Her father dropped a weighted bait line down until it touched bottom. He took a stick with the remainder of the line and pushed it into the snow, on a slant away from the hole. This would give some leverage against a crab pulling with the tide. He set another line and then he walked to Nedercook and said, "You do next two."

Nedercook was happy to do this. She lowered the rock weight, then carefully raised the rock off the bottom twice so she would have the feel of the weight and know immediately if a crab was on the next time. She secured the stick as she had seen her father do. Together they walked back to the first hole. Inerluk bent over as he put his mitten into his big parka pocket. He used the thumb and first finger of each hand to gently take up the slack until he felt the weight of the sinker. He shook his head as he let it drop back. He tried the next hole in the same manner. When the slack was taken up, Nedercook knew that he had something as he slowly continued to pull the line hand over hand. He was careful never to let the line slack or drop back, nor did he jerk it forward because if he did, the crab would suddenly let go of the bait with its big pincers and drop back to the bottom. Oolark came running with the short pole that had the hook shape, holding it ready as they strained to see down into the dark waters in the hole. As he pulled, Inerluk was careful to keep the line centered in the hole so the crab's legs were less likely to touch the ice as they hung out in all directions. It only

129

took one little touch with the tip of a leg for the crab to let go and drop back.

"I see," Oolark said, and his gloveless hand plunged into the cold water, grabbing the end of a big leg. Before he could get it out of the water the crab had opened his pincers and let the bait fall free. Oolark carried the crab a short way from the hole and placed it belly-side down. He put his mukluked foot on it and applied a pressure that killed the crab and also drained out the bluish fluid, making it much more tasty. Then he folded all the crab legs and, dragging his heel to make a long, narrow depression, he placed the crab into it. When the crab froze in this position, the legs would not be sticking out in all directions to be broken off easily.

"You try," Inerluk said to his daughter as they reached the third hole. Nedercook's heart leapt up in excitement. Taking off her mittens, she placed them in her parka pocket. Straddling the hole as best she could, she began taking up slack until the weight could be felt.

"Papa . . ." she cried excitedly, but the words she was going to say died in her mouth and came out, "Gone," because, in her excitement, she had let the line slack after a quick pull. "Put it down quick," her father advised. She dropped it until the weight touched bottom. "We leave, maybe he try again," her father said as they moved to another hole.

"Oolark, you try," her father said at the next hole. There was one on the line, but just as the men saw it, a leg touched the ice and it started to drop. Inerluk jabbed the pole with the hooked end and soon he had the crab on top of the ice. "Big one," he said as her brother lowered the line. Her father took care of the crab as Oolark had.

"Pull slow — no jerk," Inerluk said as Nedercook stooped to try a line. The crab had not been raised from the bottom very high, so it had not drifted away. It had found the bait again. This time Nedercook did not cry out, but concentrated on pulling evenly, and soon Oolark saw a crab leg. Taking no chances, he grabbed it and pulled it out of the water. It was the biggest so far. "Good big one! You fix," her father said.

Oolark went back to digging and chiseling holes while Inerluk checked the other lines. Nedercook dropped the line to the bottom and prepared the crab, nestling it in the snow. She hurried over to see what her father was pulling up. Just as she reached the hole he was grabbing a crab. He passed it to Nedercook; she danced around in joy as she said to no one in particular, "We got four."

The next check of lines brought nothing. Oolark had one hole open to water, so Nedercook scooped away the ice while her father baited the line. Looking up suddenly, Nedercook remembered her promise to her mother. "Go home, help mama," she said.

"You try holes," her father said as he went to gather the crabs for her to take home. She got one more but it was an average size. Her father put it with the others in the big mesh bag. Feeling happy, she almost hopped part of the way home.

Nedercook came bursting in, pack and all, happy that she had not forgotten to be home on time. "I remember," she said joyfully, swinging the pack down beside her mother, who sat on a caribou skin. Her legs were extended before her as she was using the light from the skylight to sew by. Nedercook watched her mother's face brighten and break into a big smile.

"Ar-nick-ka . . . kuk-kook," (crab) she said, setting aside her sewing. Nedercook proudly showed her the big crab that she had pulled to the top of the ice. Her mother knew and felt her pride. Taking the big crab, she pulled off the big pincer and set it aside, then she pulled all the legs from one side of the crab and placed them in a pot. Her mother picked up the body of the crab which had the legs attached to one side, and asked, "Want to take it to Oopick?" then, "I set skins out."

131

Nedercook gave her mother a big hug. Then holding the crab by the legs so it could easily be seen, she walked proudly to Oopick's. On the way, others old and young asked her about the crab. Oopick was not very spry any more, but happiness radiated from her wrinkled face and her praise was high for her little friend. Even though she was not a blood relative, Oopick had called her "Grandchild" for as long as she could remember. It was a custom back in those days between good friends. Nedercook called her "Grandma Oopick." As Nedercook started back she met her sister, Paniagon, on her way out to the ice to help their father catch crabs. She would help him take up the fishing gear at the end of the day and pull the sled while their father guided it over the rough places. Nedercook looked after her sister for a long moment before turning toward home.

That evening when her father and sister returned home, he set several of the nice crabs aside for Paniagon to take home; some he put on the cache, as his wife also liked frozen crab; the rest were carried into the inne. Nedercook had rubbed the skins and cooked the crab she had carried home. Her sister helped her to put more crabs in pots to cook, and before leaving had a taste of what her sister had cooked.

"Surprise Kimik," she said. Her husband was away hunting for caribou. "Maybe home tomorrow." Thanking her father, she left because she did not like walking home in the dark. Kimik had taken Komo with him, as he always did when he hunted alone. He had had Komo ever since he was a pup. Often he had tied Komo up while he was very little, because the elders told him that the dog would not fight the leash and cry if he did this early enough. Now Komo needed no leash, only his master's command. Kimik treated Komo well, and in return Komo loved him.

The villagers told a story of a man who horribly mistreated a dog. Upon death his spirit had to return as a dog and suffer the same treatment.

The crab cooked quickly and Nedercook finally had the last pot of crab boiling. She was glad this was coming to an end as her hands were tired from all the skins she had rubbed yesterday and today, and also from taking the hot cooked crabs out of the pot and putting in the prickly-shelled crabs to cook. The inne was getting dark, so it was time to light the seal oil lamp. Without warning, the crab pot boiled over. The liquid ran into the fire. Smoke and steam filled the room, making it even darker.

Nedercook, in her excitement to stop the boiling pot before it put out the fire, grabbed at the pot. It was too hot and she dropped it. As it hit the dirt floor, the boiling liquid splashed out and onto the back of her hand, causing a burn that quickly blistered her skin. Her father, who was removing his mukluk, came to help her and pulled the pot from the edge of the fire. Acting quickly, he grabbed some emergency kindling to revive the fire.

"It hurts," Nedercook cried as she went to her mother. In all this excitement they did not notice that the pot when dropped had hit a burning twig that flew and landed on the fringed part of a grass rug in front of Kiachook's bed. Suddenly flame broke out just as she was about to examine her daughter's hand. "Fire!" they cried as one. Inerluk turned and saw the flames. He grabbed his big work mitten and soon smothered the fire.

"Quick! Put hand in water," Kiachook said, passing her daughter a pot of cold water. Then she went outdoors and returned with a dipper of snow, which she put into the water. While she did this, Nedercook took her hand from the water, trying to see it in the dim light. "Put it back," Kiachook commanded, then added, "Too dark." She turned as she said this and busied herself with the lighting of the oil lamp. By its flickering light she looked at the injured hand. "Needs kug-ruk," (Alaskan

133

artemisia) she said. Remembering that they had sent their pouch of it to a friend on the far side of the village, Inerluk decided to go to the Big Dance House. It was closer.

"I go Big Dance House, get some," Inerluk said as back on went the mukluk he had removed, and out the passageway he hurried.

"Be all right," Kiachook consoled her. With an arm around her daughter, she knelt beside her until Inerluk returned.

He cut a strip of thin skin from one of the ground squirrels that Nedercook had rubbed soft that day. He called Nedercook to him as he knelt by the dim, flickering light. Using some of the finely shredded beach grass, he gently wiped the water from her hand, being careful not to touch the injured part. Then he covered the scalded area with the crumbled leaves of the plant and wrapped it gently with the thin skin. "Be all right," he comforted.

Oolark arrived later than usual. He was smiling broadly so they knew that his luck was good. His hunting sack looked full. Removing it, he placed it before his mother.

"Ar-nick-ka," she said as she pulled out a large northern or tundra hare. These averaged twelve pounds, sometimes more, and were white in winter with black tipped ears. Reaching in again, she pulled out another hare and two ptarmigans.

"You good hunter," she said proudly.

"Set two snares and little net," he said, passing off his mother's praise.

That evening everyone took pity on Nedercook and spoke comforting words to her, and she did not have to crack the crab shells for her dinner.

"I get big pincers," Oolark said, going out to get the ones their father had set near the entrance way. They did not cook these, believing that they would be stronger if they did not. After they were cleaned, these were used as toys and were tossed up in the air a few inches. With these they often played the "Ask" game. Ask any question then flip the pincer up, and if it landed so it stood on the open end, it was a strong "Yes." If it toppled over so it lay arched away from the ground, it was a questionable "Yes." If it fell in any other position it was definitely "No." All the family cleaned these and passed them to Nedercook.

After dinner Oolark skinned the two rabbits while his mother picked and cleaned the ptarmigan. She saved some of the feathers for use later when she would make clay pots, plates and bowls. She believed that the feathers strengthened the clay dishes. She preferred dog hairs when they were available.

That evening after the lamp was out, Inerluk did not wait for his daughter to ask for a story but offered to tell a long one. Maybe he knew that she would be very aware of the throbbing hand and could not fall easily to sleep. He began:

The Grandson

Once long ago after a long famine, there was left only a grandmother and her grandson. She raised him as best she could. She taught him how to carve and make spears, bows, and arrows, and how to care for the game he killed for food. She also showed him how to make a kayak.

When he had grown a little older, she told him one day to go out and try to get an animal with horns. She was very firm about warning him against trying to get a big animal without horns because at his age she did not want him to try to kill a bear. Finally, after many attempts, he was able to get an animal with horns, a caribou. At last he had grown to be a man. He would get much food for his grandmother.

With his coming to manhood, the distant cliffs to the west seemed to beckon to him until he could not resist the call any longer. He made plans to leave his grandmother with plenty of food and, although the cliffs were a long, long ways away, he had to go and see what was there. Finally on the day he was to leave in his kayak, he told his grandmother that he must find out what it was that was drawing him to the cliffs.

For many days he paddled long and hard, finally reaching the cliffs. They were very high and the water washed right up to the base, so he continued to paddle along offshore in front of the cliffs. Rounding a point of rocks, he saw before him a large village. As he paddled closer he could hear the people shouting.

"Kayak coming — visitor from up there."

When his kayak touched the beach, the people of the village rushed forth and before he could get out they picked up the kayak while he was still sitting in it. They carried kayak and man away from the water before they set the kayak down.

One man who seemed to be the chief came and said, "Take this visitor to my home." When the villagers set him down, he left his kayak where it was placed.

In all the games that followed, wrestling, high jumping, and all, the visitor excelled over all the village competitors.

One man asked the chief if the visitor could go with them to a cave. The chief nodded his consent. The visitor then followed the men to a cave where they served a big dish of bumblebees. He could not bring himself to eat from the dish, even though the others did. When they were through they all returned to the Big Dance House and the games continued.

He used all his strength and the tricks he had learned, because he knew if he lost they would kill him. He was always the winner. During the evening a woman with a big fur ruff entered the room. The ruff was made from both wolf and wolverine, an indication that the family was rich (which meant a good hunter in the family).She asked where Kar-ar-nark man was, meaning the man from up there. When she was shown who he was, she approached and asked him to go with her. Next morning when he woke up, he found that he was in a grave with a dead skeleton. (Eskimos in those days built graves above ground because the ground was usually frozen too hard to dig with their primitive tools, so they used driftwood to make an above-ground enclosure.)

When he returned to the village he told them what had happened. They said that she was a woman who had picked the salmonberries after they had turned white. She had died last summer, but her spirit was still earthbound. Then the villagers tried to get the better of him in more games, but he was always the winner. After this he was favored by the chief.

Soon he married the chief's daughter.

Later he remembered his grandmother and decided he should visit her, so he started back in a skin boat with his wife and some of her family. They found his grandmother alive and well. He was glad. His grandmother was glad there were other people living beside them. The grandson told her of the people of the village and said he did not know there could be so many people in the world. As the years passed there was much visiting back and forth between his grandmother's place and the village.

Inerluk paused when he finished telling the story, then he added, "Hand will get well."

CHAPTER 19

OOPICK DIES

The cold, dark, and often stormy days of winter were passing and then, after one very stormy day, Oopick was found dead in her bed. Kiachook did what she could to clean her face and straighten her hair. Oopick had reached the very old, old age when dark hairs start to grow in to replace the gray. It was said this happened to the very, very old and that their eyesight also begins to improve after a certain age. Inerluk and his sons, along with other men of the village, gathered wood for her grave.

Nedercook felt great loss and deep sadness. Oopick looked so small and wrinkled, and although Nedercook looked at Oopick's face, the crinkly smile did not come.

The men placed Oopick in the grave with her few most treasured belongings. They did not cut the fur ruff from Oopick's parka, because it was hers. If it had been a ruff that was loaned to her, they would cut it off and return it to the lender at this time. As they built the crude shelter about her body to keep the dogs and animals away, tears rolled down Nedercook's cheeks. She could not stop them. Kiachook said nothing, but put her arm around her daughter for a little while. She knew that some grieving and tears were healthy.

That evening, and for the next six nights, villagers brought food and gathered in the Big Dance House, to eat and sing. There was some dancing to celebrate

Oopick's departure to the spirit world. Kiachook let Nedercook cry without restraint for the first day, nor did she say anything to stop the sniffling and sobs during the first night. On the afternoon of the second day, as the evening approached, she walked to where Nedercook stood rubbing red eyes, and placing an arm gently around her shoulders said, "You have cried enough. Now it is time to stop, for they say that too many tears will but wet the grave of the departed. She suffers not, but she would be saddened to see you so unhappy." After a brief silence Kiachook added, "Daughter, when grief comes into your life, try hard to keep doing the things you are used to doing, and eat as you always have. If you don't eat and work, it will want to become a habit and it will be much harder for you later on." Then she looked into her daughter's red eyes as she said, "We will go to the Big Dance House tonight and give our help to the others who are celebrating Oopick's admission to the spirit world." Kiachook added, "Sometimes the spirit of a person will not leave and it becomes what we call Earthbound Spirit. This is to be pitied."

The early days of spring passed quickly with Kiachook teaching Nedercook all she could, praising her when she was deserving, keeping quiet when she thought she could do better, but quick to correct if she saw her making a mistake.

Some of the village women, like Oopick, had dark lines tatooed on their chins. Usually there was one vertical line in the center, but some had three lines; these were always below the lower lip and stopped above the end of the chin. Nedercook said that when she grew older she was going to have three vertical lines on her chin, but for now she would settle for a dark line going around her wrist, like a bracelet. Her mother gave her permission. Today Paniagon would do it during brightest sunlight.

A thin bone needle and twisted sinew were on hand, with the darkest charcoal. The needle pierced a small, pinched section of wrist skin and followed just below the skin for a very short distance. Darkest charcoal was rubbed all along the sinew and then it was drawn through. This was repeated until Nedercook had a dark line nearly two inches long. The pain was extreme and she asked Paniagon to stop. This cured her of wanting any future chin markings, and the wrist line was never lengthened. (This practice should not be attempted by anyone of this generation because it is likely to cause infection and injury.)

CHAPTER 20
BARTER

One day while snow still covered all of the land, but the sun was starting to thaw little spots on the sunny side, two men walked into the village. They were from the village of Na-chiv-vic (White Mountain). They brought a verbal invitation from their chief to come to their village celebration. This celebration was held once a year. Each year it was held at a different village just before traveling got too difficult because of the melting snow. This year it would be held on the Fish River.

The gathering of different villages together in the early spring was a custom practiced by many villages during Nedercook's childhood. Two men were dispatched by the elders to each of the invited villages. The invited would either walk, pulling a sled carrying gifts, or go by dog team, a sled with a few dogs helping to pull. Not many people, perhaps two or three families, had dogs back in Nedercook's time, because dogs required much food that people could use. At times this food might be needed to get a family through the winter. So it was only the good hunter who sometimes kept a dog. If a dog team was needed, it would be formed by using all the dogs from a village.

Visitors who came on invitation would gather at the host village's Big Dance House. There would be much feasting for everyone. Then the people of the village that had sent the invitation would sing, and in their song they would describe what they would like to receive from the visitors.

142

Then came the visitors' turn to sing and they told the villagers what they would like to receive as gifts. Expensive gifts such as fur parkas were exchanged at these meetings. The visitors would stay one or two nights and then return home. Their sled would be filled with the exchange gifts, such as mukluks, parkas, wooden dishes, bed robes, and other prized objects.

This year Inerluk decided to remain at home. Last year he had taken Nutchuk with him. It was the first time Nutchuk had been away from his village on a trading mission. They had gone up the coast to Solomon and stayed two nights. The trip gave Nutchuk a chance to see other people, mingle, and know the feeling of being a visitor.

"You go this time," Inerluk said to Nutchuk after the invitation came; then he added, "Next year take Oolark." A big smile was on his face as he said this. He purposely avoided Oolark's gaze because he knew that Oolark did not like singing in public. "He older by then," added his father.

Word spread through the village that Nutchuk would be taking Inerluk's place this year. Excitement stirred the villagers as they brought gifts to the home of Inerluk, along with their requests for what they wished in exchange. Five other men from the village were also going. Each man had a certain number of gifts to take along, with the responsibility for the requested exchanges. The person responsible for an exchange gift had to sing a song at the gathering before all the strangers of the village. The song included the name of the person sending the gift, a description of the gift, and the desired exchange. He was responsible for making as favorable an exchange as possible.

Nedercook wanted her brother to bring back a flint arrowhead, because for years she had heard of the great fight that had occurred by the Fish River, above the village of White Mountain. It was told that a group of

Indians had come to attack the Eskimos. Many were killed on both sides, but the Indians finally retreated. For years after, arrows and arrowheads were found where this great battle had taken place.

Many villagers and children turned out early to see the six men leave with the two sleds. One of the sleds belonged to Inerluk, so Nutchuk could choose two men as his companions. Each man had the packs he was responsible for, along with food for the trail, and his personal belongings.

After the men departed, Oolark and his father went fishing for crab. Nedercook stayed home to help her mother. There was much scraping of caribou legs to be done, skins to be tanned, and mukluks to be made. In between this work Nedercook also tended the cooking pots. The scraping was hard work and she could feel herself perspiring as she did this. The skylight was open but it did not provide much fresh air. This handwork was very tiring but she did not complain; she knew she was helping her mother with things that her sister had done uncomplainingly for years. "You sing," her mother said, "Learn new song." Nedercook listened to her mother sing the words:

Woman Has
Seal Poke Of Fish
I heard of a woman
who has a seal poke
full of prepared fish in oil.
What has she used for a kayak?
Her hands have been used for this.

"Short one," her mother said as she finished singing. Then, as they both rubbed skins, Nedercook sang the song as closely as she could, getting in all of the "A-yong-eeh-yays." These phrases were in most of the songs, filling in the song and carrying on the tune.

It was customary for the children of the village to learn

144

all the songs, stories, and legends that were told or sung to them, because the Rocky Point Eskimos did not have a written language. They depended upon the memories of the children as they grew older to carry on the songs and legends so they would not be lost for future generations. Therefore, the stories had to be memorized and memorized correctly. The bedtime stories were also lessons, because the next day Nedercook would repeat last night's story to either a parent or an elder. Any mistakes were always corrected.

The evening dusk descended without mother or daughter being aware of it. They were trying to finish the last round of squirrel skins, busily rubbing the skins over and over again until the pelts were soft and dry, then pushing them onto stretchers for the last time. The skins would be left thus overnight to rid them of any moisture. In the morning they could be sewn into garments or tied in bundles and stored.

As they were thus occupied, Paniagon came upon them. "Ar-nick-ka," she exclaimed as she stood in the entrance way, looking at them in the dim light. "Why no light?" she questioned.

"Too busy," her mother replied. They had been too intent upon their work to notice the dimming light.

"I make some for you," Paniagon said as she passed a bowl of Eskimo ice cream to her mother.

"Quana," Kiachook said happily as she took and held the bowl in both of her hands. When she had it safely on her lap she used her index finger to scoop up a finger full. "Ummm, nuk-goo (good). Daughter, taste it," she said, turning her head in Nedercook's direction.

Nedercook came to kneel by her mother's side. She liked the moss berries that were in the ice cream. Her sister, in the meantime, had taken a light from the coals to light the seal oil lamp. Suddenly it seemed very light in the inne. Kiachook offered the bowl to Paniagon but Paniagon shook her head.

"Keep tasting," she said with a smile. Then she added, "I go before too dark."

"Quana," her mother called after her.

Shortly after, Oolark and Inerluk returned. The big mesh bag was full of crabs and there were more on the sled. Oolark spotted the ice cream and took a big finger full.

"Paniagon make it," his mother said proudly.

That evening it was Nedercook's turn to tell what she had learned, as she would do after memorizing anything new. As she sang "Woman Has a Seal Poke of Fish" her parents listened. They knew where every word should

146

be. Nedercook sang it correctly. Her mother listened carefully, smiling her pride in the darkness.

Time passed swiftly as each day of early spring brought more light and the nights became shorter. Now the village was filled with excitement as expectation grew for the return of the men with the exchange gifts.

One day before dark they returned. That evening the villagers gathered at the Big Dance House, sitting in semi-circles on the floor. The men who had taken exchange gifts came from the opening to stand before the crowd. In turn they announced the name of the person who had sent a gift with them, and the name of the gift brought back. Then from their bags they produced the exchange gift for that person.

Among some families there was much rejoicing, while others thought, next year we will make a big gift to send.

CHAPTER 21

NEDERCOOK'S BIRTH

Inerluk seldom allowed himself the luxury of reflection during the precious daylight hours, but today he had already hunted in the morning and brought meat home. This afternoon he was going out on the ice to fish for tomcod just as soon as his little daughter gathered together her fishing gear. As he sat waiting he remembered Nedercook's birth.

Over ten years ago Kiachook had complained about a lump in her abdomen. It seemed she had carried it for over three years and no child had grown from it. People said she was too old to bear more children. He remembered how she had grown restless. It was then that they had agreed to go and see one of the wise men of their village. They were the prophets, the healers. A person went to one of them when in trouble. The term used in those days was almost like "miracle men."

This lump was beyond Kiachook's control for it did not change. It lay inert as a long upright lump, not the normal shape for a pregnant woman. For a time she had listened to the others in the village; they said, "Kiachook too old to bear children." Yes, they were both old, but Kiachook was dissatisfied with the advice of these women.

Inerluk remembered that the miracle man had told his wife to lie on her back while Inerluk sat on a log nearby. The miracle man placed his hands over the lump. Then he moved his gentle hands and carefully felt the bump and all of its outline. Then, with his hands still moving gently over the lump, he began chanting his message. His voice rose and fell as he asked, "This still, quiet, lifeless form held captive in this woman's womb — may it this day be given the spirit of life to grow — and come into this world of the living as a special child favored by the miracle men."

As the months passed the lump began to change and later Kiachook felt the movement of life. Inerluk remembered their joy.

They moved from the village to their summer camp to be near the good berry patches and to where salmon passed close to the beach on their migration.

It was at this summer camp on a bright, sunny day in August that little Nedercook was born, outdoors on the beach beside a large log. As was the custom then, after the birth Kiachook arose and stepped upon the small pebbles. In winter small pebbles were placed upon the floor for the first steps of a mother after giving birth, but here the pebbles were all over so she did not have to bother with that.

In celebration of the baby's birth Oopick, being the oldest woman of their village, would have the privilege of asking them for whatever food she wanted. This was the custom when a baby was born.

Years later when Nedercook could talk, she told her parents about the brightness that hurt her eyes, and of the big log that lay beside her. She remembered nothing else of that day.

About that time of year the villagers gathered the low salmon-colored berries that grew on the hillsides, those they called salmonberries. A smile lingered on Inerluk's face as he remembered how beautiful they thought this little girl child was, how her mother had gathered the berries so her milk would carry the good, strength-giving fluid that would nourish this robust child.

"Papa, papa, I am ready," Inerluk's thoughts were interrupted as Nedercook came bursting from the inne, clad in parka and mukluks.

Inerluk slipped his pack over his shoulder. He decided against carrying his daughter's, knowing she would take pride in carrying her own. They did not have far to go to reach the hole he had cut yesterday. Nedercook quickly cleared the ice from the hole and dropped her line in. The line was wrapped around two sticks. Nedercook held one in each hand, about two feet apart. Then like an expert she wrapped the line around her left stick a couple of times and began to jig with her right hand. When she caught a fish she would raise her right hand, and then with her left she would catch the line with her short stick and pull it up. As she did this, her right hand would bring the end of her short fishing stick under to catch the line and bring it up, repeating this until the fish was up on top of the ice. She would then release the fish from the hook and drop the line back into the water. With the short stick she would quickly kill the tomcod. She had been taught early to kill things quickly, never to let anything suffer.

They fished until the quiet darkness began to settle about them. It was time to gather the fish, at least twenty pounds. Inerluk shouldered the pack and they headed home.

"Papa, can I go tell them what we got?" Nedercook asked as they drew close.

"Yes, go," he said gently. As he watched her run he indulged in one small chuckle, for he knew the family would be aware of their return. He could see the flicker of the outdoor cooking light. They would see her coming on ahead and all go inside before she got there, and be busy about other things. She would burst excitedly upon them and say, "Come see what we caught!"

When Inerluk came close enough to see the cooking fire he could smell the pot of seal meat. The fire was reduced to coals by now, but the pot still simmered. Kiachook had let the fire die down to save wood, because it was the woman's job to gather the small pieces of wood for the cooking fire.

The family gathered around the glowing coals by the steaming pot. The chill in the air on that calm evening did not disturb anyone as they filled their plates with hot food. The stars twinkled brightly overhead while the moon rose slowly above the horizon, turning lighter as the minutes passed and sending down a soft light to fall about the quiet people, whose only sound was that of eating. It was such a calm evening that Inerluk turned open the skylight. He carried the last of the glowing coals indoors and placed them in the indentation dug into the ground and surrounded by rocks. It was in the center of the room. This was where Kiachook usually cooked when the weather was too cold, or if she was busy working at something and still wanted to keep an eye on the cooking.

The dim moonlight, filtered through the skylight, plus the glowing coals, gave the room and Nedercook a warm, secure feeling as she prepared for bed.

"Papa, are you too tired to tell me a story?" she asked.

Inerluk was silent for a few moments as he thought about the difference this child was making in their lives, and how the stories he had told to each of his older children seemed to take on new importance as he repeated them to little Nedercook. "It will be the story of the shrew," he said. He began:

The Shrew

Once a shrew or mole heard someone singing, "Shrew, shrew, he has very short hair." So the shrew replied, "Ha, ha, my grandmother made my hair very

short so when I travel in stormy weather it will not matt up." Then the song continued, "Shrew, shrew, why do you have such short legs?" The shrew replied, "Ha, ha, my grandmother made them short so that if I am traveling on slippery ice in a big wind I shall not blow away."

The song continued again, "Shrew, shrew, why was your nose so long and skinny?"

He replied, "Ha, ha, my grandmother made my nose long and thin so that if I am sometimes hungry and I come across a seal poke tied up tight, it will be small enough that I can still sip a little of its contents and not starve." Still the song persisted, "Shrew, shrew, why are your teeth the color that they are, as if they have been burnt or scorched?" To this there was no answer. Only the sounds of a crying or weeping shrew were heard.

CHAPTER 22
SEAL HUNTING

Next morning the two brothers decided to go seal
hunting. They checked the weather as their
father had taught them. This was the time of
year when the seals lay on top of the ice, sunning themselves in the hot spring sunshine. They raised their heads
to look around; if nothing was moving they would lie
down again. If they raised their heads and caught the
movement of a hunter — flip! — almost before you
could make a move, the seal would be down a hole and
out of sight. This time of year the sun shone bright and
hot, reflecting from ice and snow a burning, tanning,
snow-blinding brightness as the days lengthened. The
sun melted the snow in spots to make little fresh water
pools on top of the salty sea ice.

Nutchuk and Oolark climbed over several pressure
ridges, heading for the highest peak of ice, and then sat
close together so their elbows practically touched. They
were wearing primitive eye pieces to protect themselves
from snow blindness. (The eye pieces consisted of two
pieces of bone or wood, with small horizontal slits to
see through. The pieces were attached to each other at
the nose with rawhide and tied to the person's head.
Others were made of one front piece with slits and tied
to the head. Snow blindness was a very painful thing;
one would have to stay in the dark part of the inne for
three or more days until the eyes recovered.)

Oolark saw a dark spot on the ice to the left and
nudged his brother, who looked and nodded his head.
Both knew that the less they talked while hunting, the

better their chances. Oolark was looking at the dark line and could barely see one end rise a little, when, ever so gently, his brother gave his elbow two nudges. Years of hunting had taught them not to make sudden moves while watching for game, but each man was capable of great speed and quick movements when it was necessary.

Ever so slowly Oolark turned his head to the right, just in time to see a seal's head come out of the ice. It poked its head high and looked about two or three times, sinking back out of sight each time. Then it crawled out onto the ice, flipped a little, and lay still.

They saw there was no cover close to the seal. A little to the left there was some rough ice, enough to hide them if they were careful.

"We try," whispered Nutchuk as they waited for the seal to drop back to sleep. Quickly they were off the high ice and each froze in position before the seal looked up. Bit by bit they worked their way around until the ice was between them and the seal, then they crept forward on hands and knees. There was no more concealment. For a short time they looked, then Nutchuk motioned with his hand that his shorter brother should try. Oolark was wearing his lightest-colored clothing for hunting on the ice. Nutchuk watched his brother. He was doing well — if only he could make it another hundred feet. As Oolark started forward from his crouched position, another seal suddenly poked its head up a few feet in front of him. It made a sound as it ducked out of sight. This must have warned the sleeping seal, for it raised its head and caught the surprised Oolark in movement. He stopped to crouch too late. The seal disappeared.

Nutchuk quickly came forward and silently indicated that Oolark should stand guard at the first hole, while he hurried on to the sleeping seal's empty hole. They knew that either the first seal or another one passing just might try to poke its head out again. When Nutchuk reached the sleeping seal's hole he looked back at Oolark and saw that he was ready to thrust his spear on a moment's notice. Almost an hour passed while the brothers stood like two statues, poised to strike.

Then Oolark saw a very slight change in the water hole. The water rose and fell ever so slightly. He tensed as his grip tightened on his spear. Soon there was more movement in the water and he knew that a seal was about to surface. He saw the nostrils first, and as he jabbed the spear with all his strength, he saw its head. He knew he had made a hit. The spear point came free from the shaft. The attached rawhide held fast. Nutchuk came running and together they pulled the mammal from the water. The seal was speared through the nose.

"Young be happy," Nutchuk said as he looked at it. Oolark knew that a ban was placed on ball playing, to be lifted only when a hunter speared a seal in the nose. They took their places again for a time longer, but no more seals came.

They decided to return early enough that the children could have some fun that evening. As they began to climb the hillside in front of the village, children, anxious to know whether the ban was lifted, ran down to meet them, just as they had run to meet all the other lucky hunters before them.

The children's joyful shouts alerted the villagers. When the two brothers dragged the seal through the village, the restrictions on ball playing were automatically lifted. Children appeared carrying their balls. Once again the happy squeals and laughter of the children were heard.

That evening, as soon as she could, Nedercook took the nice new ball Paniagon had made and given her at the big festival. It was one of the better balls, made from caribou skin and filled with the hairs of the caribou. Her ball was light and bouncy. The balls of some of the other children were made with thicker leather and filled with finely scraped wood shavings. She joined the children below the village, where the ground was beginning to show through here and there. It was the flattest area.

This was the time of year for hunting seals and oogruk. The Inerluk brothers decided to go out the next morning. Open water was visible from the village, and they knew the animals liked to swim along the edge of the open water and sleep on the ice. Nedercook asked if she could go but her brothers refused, saying that if the ice went out they would have enough trouble getting themselves back to shore.

They decided to take the kayak today, so they stored some food in it along with their primitive gear and plenty of rawhide. They put the kayak on the little sled with ivory runners, a sled made especially for the kayak. The brothers checked the ice, as their father would, before leaving the shore. About halfway out to the open water, at a point where their father could see it from where he was working on a net, they stood a pole up. It was about five feet tall. This they would call a marker for help. The sun was hot and the reflected rays from the snow and water burned their faces and hands even darker.

This was a good year for game. They could see several seals and oogruks. Back in those days, when game was plentiful it was much more tame, perhaps because of the Eskimo's quiet method of hunting. Oolark and Nutchuk pulled the kayak as near to the water as they could and still keep it hidden behind a pile of rough ice. Taking their spears, they climbed to the top of a pressure ridge and peeked over.

Two seals were swimming in the water; farther out, an oogruk was swimming and diving. To the right, a few seals lay about on a little open area of ice. To their left they saw what hunters of their day always hoped to see and seldom did — two oogruks, a harpooner's perfect targets. The pressure ridge they were on continued in an angle until it was near the triangular

156

piece of ice. They looked it over carefully.

While they were looking out to sea they saw a long, dark line above the water and knew right away that the murres were coming back. The birds arrive annually around April 5 to 10. When they first arrive, they fish and fly in large groups, gathering by the hundreds, swimming and diving in the open water. Within a few weeks they fly in smaller flocks during the evenings, toward the high cliffs, approaching them to within a quarter of a mile or less, then veering sharply and flying back to the water. Flock after flock will go through this ritual for a few weeks, flying closer and closer to the cliff each evening. Then, as if by signal, they will all rest on the cliff overnight, but leave after sunup in the morning.

The two brothers were happy to see the birds return, but they did not sing songs to the new arrivals, as the women of the village did. With the coming of the murres, the eider ducks and the oldsquaw ducks were also on the open water. The sounds of the murres splash-landing in the water, and their calls filling the air, seemed to help as the two brothers worked their way along the back side of the pressure ridge until they were directly behind the two oogruks.

They both knew they would be lucky to get one oogruk, but the brothers were daring and resourceful hunters. They were willing to take a chance if there was something to be gained, so they devised a plan. Nutchuk, being the taller and the faster runner, would try to get the oogruk nearer the water. His brother would try for the closer one.

Being careful and quiet, they crept forward until they were behind the piece of triangular ice readying their spears and themselves. Then a slight nod of Nutchuk's head and both sprang forward. Oolark went to the right, his brother to the left of the triangle of ice. Oolark's oogruk was so close. He thrust with all his strength as he rounded the ice triangle. Nutchuk rushed toward the other oogruk, which had not made a hole in the ice but had crawled onto it from the open water. He flung his spear with all the force he had. The spear went deep, but the oogruk rolled into the water and dived out of sight. As it did so, the inflated seal poke tied to the end of the rawhide and fastened to the spearhead was dragged into the water. Nutchuk turned to look at his brother. The oogruk lay beside Oolark on the ice. The spear had plunged into the back of the neck in the area of the spinal cord. Both brothers had happy smiles. While Oolark rolled his oogruk farther from the hole, Nutchuk went for the kayak. The inflated seal poke was bobbing some 50 feet away.

The brothers quickly put the kayak into the water. Oolark steadied it while his brother got in. Nutchuk paddled out to the inflated seal poke, took the pole with the hook on the end, and hooked the rawhide. Then he fastened a strong line to the rawhide that held the bobbing seal poke. He paddled back to the ice. He said, "Next time we leave *long* rawhide tied to poke." Oolark took the line and tied it to the triangle of ice. Then he offered to run back to the marker and put a dark parka over it.

Inerluk was busy working on the net, but as he worked he kept looking out to sea for a signal. He looked up as he had a hundred times before. His eyes caught movement, one of the sons traveling fast, reaching the pole post and leaving a dark object. The figure started back from where it had come.

Inerluk picked up his net and took it indoors; one never left something like that out where dogs could eat it.

"Sons need help," he said to his wife and daughter, "I go with sled." He continued, "Nedercook go to Kimik, tell him."

"Can I come out?" Nedercook asked her father.

"After you tell him," he said as he started out the door.

158

Nedercook grabbed her parka and mittens and was right behind him on her way to Kimik's. Breathlessly she burst upon them. Paniagon was preparing to go fishing. Kimik was repairing a broken spear. Everyone became excited. All rushed out the door. Kimik got his sled and rawhide and the three were off. For an expectant mother, Paniagon traveled fast.

Inerluk traveled swiftly and they did not catch up to him until they reached the pressure ridge, where they could see the young men cutting up one oogruk. They saw the rawhide line and the seal poke floating in the water. For a few minutes they did quite a lot of talking.

Then Nutchuk said, "We got one in water." He drew on the line, bringing the seal poke to the edge of the ice. Soon the oogruk was visible. Oolark jabbed his spear into it to make sure it would not get away. With some struggle they finally got a stronger line tied to the oogruk. Everyone took the line and pulled and pulled until it was out of the water. After exclaiming over it, the two brothers began to skin and cut it up, while Inerluk and his daughters loaded the first one into the sled he had brought.

When the second one was ready, it was put into Kimik's sled. The skin went in first with the bloody side up, then the meat was piled on along with inner parts. All washed their hands, then the kayak was lashed to the little sled with ivory runners.

Nedercook looked out to sea. Seals were swimming about and the ducks and the murres were making much commotion as they splashed in the water. The sun felt warm and friendly. It was such a beautiful, peaceful sight, one that would remain with her, returning again and again to haunt her childhood memories.

Nutchuk and his father took one sled, Kimik and Oolark the other, while the sisters brought the kayak. When they reached the pressure ridges, all the men helped one sled and then the other over it, and last the

159

kayak. As they started on again there was much giggling and laughing between Nedercook and her sister as they pulled, pushed and guided the kayak over the ice. Inerluk had picked up the signal parka on the way out to the kill.

By late sunset they made it to the beach. They took the shoreline to the bottom of the incline below the village. All slowed considerably as they started up the hill. Fellow villagers came running to help them as far as Inerluk's home. Some of the not so good hunters decided they would go hunting the next day.

Kiachook had made a fire outdoors and was by the big cooking pots. The expression on her face showed joy. She moved about like a young woman — here were two sleds of food. She was never afraid to show her joy, affection or appreciation. She threw her arms about her two sons, her husband, and then her daughters. Raising her head, she looked skyward as she said, "Quana, quana." Her thanks were words of deep gratitude, meant for a kind and all-giving spirit of the universe.

Then, as if remembering, she said, "I cooked." As she moved toward the pots, her family moved with her. Everyone had been so busy and excited that food had been forgotten. As they approached they were pleased to see that she had carried out bowls and plates for everyone.

Dusk was falling by the time they finished eating. The two brothers told of their experiences for the benefit of their mother.

"I come help tomorrow," Paniagon said as she and Kimik left, with Komo pulling a sled carrying oogruk parts. Most of the meat was put on the cache for the night, some in the first entrance way, and some the sons took with them to the Big Dance House.

Kiachook knew that her husband had put forth much energy on this day, so she decided to tell Nedercook a story while her husband rested.

I will tell you about your grandmother, who is no longer living. She was not as tall as I am, but she was a good woman and a good sewer. She made little stitches like Paniagon, not big, careless stitches like mine. She always tried to sew and help the less fortunate whenever she could. She used to tell me, "Anytime you help somebody, it is not lost, someday it comes back to you."

She used to say to us children, "Don't make fun of old people because one day you too will be old. And do not make fun or ridicule people, because if you do it will someday come back to you."

When your grandmother was a young girl our village would be visited by little men — they were not very tall. When I put my arm straight out in front of me and look straight ahead from the tip of my nose to the tip of my finger, it would be nearly a hand taller than they were. (Her mother's estimate was a bit under three feet.) These little men possessed great strength. Though I was young, I can still remember how their little tracks looked. There is one woman we knew in the village of Nome; this woman claimed that the little men had once come to her home. One of them was determined to become familiar with her. She was afraid to say no, but she started to resist his hands and realized that the little man possessed great strength. So she gave up any resistance and let him have his way. Afterwards she knew he had not only unusual muscular strength, but his male part also swelled to such a size that it was painful to her and caused her loss of blood.

Kiachook paused in her reminiscence and as she did she was conscious of the deep, steady breathing of her two companions. Sighing, she rolled over to invite sleep.

CHAPTER 23
BABY

Kiachook had barely fallen asleep, it seemed, when someone was gently shaking her shoulder. First she thought she was dreaming, then she heard Kimik's low voice, "Come, Paniagon say maybe baby come." Kiachook awoke immediately, quickly dressed in the dark, then followed Kimik out of the inne.

When Nedercook awoke the next morning she found she was alone. She dressed quickly, thinking how strange it was because as a rule she was the first one to wake up. She ran to the little knoll above the inne to see whether she could see any of her family from there. She saw her father coming from the village and ran to meet him.

"Got granddaughter," he said, then added, "Kimik come late, get your mother."

"Can I go see?" she asked eagerly.

Her father nodded his head and she was off running. Paniagon was up. She had already crossed on the small pebbles which her mother had put on the floor.

Back in those days it was customary for a girl to be named after any woman who had died in the past year or so; a boy was named after a man in the same manner.

"We call her Oopick," Paniagon said, looking at her sister. Then picking up the small bundle, she let Nedercook hold it. Nedercook looked at the little wrinkled face and smiled. Surely this could be Oopick. Suddenly she was happy. She knew that the people of her village always loved the children; they cuddled, held, and sang to them a lot while they were young, praised them, and gave them pet names. She would be able to hold little Oopick often. After the baby grew older, Paniagon would want her to eat more solid foods. She would chew part of her food until it was soft and fine, and then she would feed it to the baby, until she could eat like adults did. A child was never ignored; it knew love and caring from the time it was born.

"We go home now. Let Paniagon sleep," it was her mother who interrupted her thoughts. Gently she put little Oopick down on Paniagon's bed. Then she put her arms around her sister and said, "Happy for you." Paniagon gave back a hug, then went to her bed.

During breakfast that morning Nedercook's brothers said, "Ice go soon. We hunt today." After they left she helped her mother and father cut and care for the oogruks. Inerluk hung the heavy pieces to dry. Kiachook filled seal pokes with blubber which would render of its own into oil. These were stored in the stormy day room, because it was now too hot outdoors for storing oil. The warm, gentle breeze was perfect for drying meat. The family busied themselves with the oogruk through the day, until Paniagon came. She was carrying little Oopick in the hood of her parka, using a long belt to tie around her. The belt went over Paniagon's right

163

shoulder and under the baby's seat, then under Paniagon's left arm, and tied in front of her chest. This was the standard way of carrying children. As Paniagon sat on a log, Nedercook had to stop and peak at the baby. Then both grandparents did the same. Kiachook brought a pot of freshly cooked oogruk from the fire and said, "We eat."

Evening brought the hunters home. One pulled a seal, the other the kayak. Kimik also pulled a seal. They came to Inerluk's knowing Paniagon would be there. Nedercook liked having a fire outdoors. She put on a couple more pieces of wood to make it look cheerful as the hunters approached. Happiness showed on their faces.

"Tomorrow we fish for tomcod," Kiachook told Nedercook, because the ice would soon be gone and it would not be back until fall. Fishing was good now. Others of the village were seen on the ice every day, fishing close to the beach.

That evening, since Inerluk had worked on two oogruk windpipes during the day, preparing them for leather, he decided to repeat to Nedercook one of the old, old, beliefs of the village. Back then a woman's sewing kit was even more primitive than Nedercook's. Nedercook's sewing kit was a circular gut bag with a drawstring at the top. Inside were bone needles, a skin thimble and usually a small ulu. The kit her father described was just a piece of skin wrapped around some bone needles and a piece of tough skin for a thimble.

If a man out hunting should happen to see one of those sewing kits lying on the ground, he was warned never, never, ever to pick it up, because he just might change into a woman.

If a woman out walking or picking berries should see a piece of a man's spear — leave it alone — or she might change into a man.

These objects seem to have a strong hold over the

viewer; he is seized by a great desire to pick it up.

I saw one once, long ago, but I had been warned so I knew of this belief. I did not pick it up. For they say of these things, that if one knows of the belief it is easier to resist the desire to pick it up. Knowing this, it will give you strength so you can step away from it. If you stoop down and look, you will see that it does not touch the ground, but hovers just a little above it.

There is a legend about a man who lived at Top-Kuk. He had two wives. Years and years ago, some men who were good hunters had two wives. Most men could not afford two wives, so it became standard to have only one wife.

One day this man left his home to go hunting. He climbed a little knoll where he would be able to look down and out across the sea. He was hoping to spot a seal from this higher place. As he glanced down he saw a sewing kit on the ground near him. Without thinking, he picked it up. He returned to his home — and then there were three women living in that house.

When her father finished Nedercook thought how advanced her people were to have a real sewing kit.

Next morning Nedercook's two brothers and Kimik left to go hunting. They took the kayak because they would be at the water's edge.

Nedercook carried the fishing gear for her mother and herself. Kiachook liked to get out and fish in the warm sunshine. She carried her walking stick whenever she was going any distance from the inne these days. It served three purposes: to help her on slippery places, to check where she was going when the footing was uncertain over thin ice, and to help when water covered a soft bottom. When footing was doubtful she would jab her stick in front as she cautiously chose her steps. When footing was safe the stick barely touched ground. She traveled fast.

Happily she took her place near Nedercook. Other women were scattered over the ice, all fishing. The women differed from the men in that, when knowing there was no other game to scare away, they laughed and talked as they fished. But they did not stomp their feet, because that would scare the fish. In general, they had a good time. They would exclaim over an extra large or small fish. Sometimes they exchanged fishing holes or told stories.

Nedercook's mother and other women of her village would always stop what they were doing and sing a song to the first bird of any species when it returned in the spring. Each kind was welcomed with a different song. Nedercook and her mother were happily fishing when they heard the call of a gull. Looking seaward, they saw two birds flying. Kiachook stopped fishing and so did the others, who knew the words of the gull song, and together they sang to the gulls.

By the time Inerluk came with the sled they had a load of fish for him. When he returned the second time it was getting late, so they helped him load the fish. Paniagon joined them earlier. She and Kiachook walked behind with Inerluk, because Nedercook wanted to take the sled back alone. Nedercook pushed, pulled, laughed, slipped and giggled her way back to the beach. Then her father said, "I help." Together they got it up the incline to the inne.

The sisters built a fire outdoors and put on some pots of fish to cook, using part sea and part fresh water. They all gutted and strung the fish on pieces of rawhide about six feet long. These they tied and hung over a pole on the drying rack, forming a half circle on each side of the pole.

Long after sundown that evening the hunters returned. The days were getting so long now that it did not get totally dark, especially during the time of the full moon. Kimik had managed to get an oogruk; the brothers, a seal each. One had to pull the kayak and the other two each pulled a seal. The oogruk took all three. Thus they had worked their way to the shore. There they had left the oogruk with Kimik's spear across it, a sign that they would soon be back. "We go back first, then eat." They took off in the dwindling light. Without anything else to pull, the three could pull the oogruk back easily. They would go to Kimik's inne. Paniagon was happy. Her mother told Nedercook to go with her sister and carry one of the pots of cooked fish.

Nedercook waited at Paniagon's for her brothers and then returned with them.

That evening it was Nedercook who repeated a story. She had been too busy all day to tell it to anyone. Her mother made two corrections and then said, "Tomorrow you tell it right." She did not say this as a reprimand. It was said as encouragement. Tomorrow she would have it right.

CHAPTER 24

CATCHING MURRES

The murres had been flying nearer and nearer to the cliff each night. Now they were roosting there, and flying back to the open water after sunup. The reason they waited so long was that the nights were still freezing. Sitting overnight on the cold, bare rocks made them so cold they could not fly until the sun warmed them.

On this morning, long before sunup, Nedercook, with her two brothers and her father, traveled along the coastal ice by dim light, reaching the cliffs by early daylight. Each carried a stick two to three feet long. Inerluk also carried a small drum. The two brothers carried their spears.

When they were below the first high cliffs where the murres were overnighting, the children spread out, roughly fifty feet apart. They were about three hundred feet from the cliff.

Inerluk walked until he was standing on a higher piece of ice. He turned and gave a nod to his children.

"Boom, boom," went his drum. He quickly put it down.

Startled, the murres naturally tried to fly but they were too cold. They fell fluttering to the ice and started running and flapping their wings, headed for the open water. Their movements at the beginning were slow. Inerluk and his children began a wild chase, catching some. The children had been taught early how to use the stick, so no living thing would be left injured or suffer. As soon as one murre was taken care of, it was dropped into the packsack and the fast chase of the second one began. Most of the time the second one would outrun them, as by then it would have warmed up, so it was generally just a wild chase.

They walked around the next projection of rocks and repeated the drum beat and chase. By the time they had gone around the third point of rocks, the sun was up enough to warm the murres, so most of them flew past the hunters a few feet off the ice.

Of those that fell, Nedercook got only two. This was her first year at this. Most of the birds were too lively and escaped her. It had been an exciting morning. They headed home with hungry appetites.

Kiachook was pleased. After breakfast she and Nedercook skinned and cleaned the birds, saving even the skin on the neck and head. They did not pick the feathers because the diving sea birds had tough skins that were used for parkas. The thicker, feathered part was used for the body of the parka, while the skin of the necks and heads was used for the hood and under the arms. Maybe this spring they would get enough to finish a parka for Inerluk.

Nedercook gathered wood and kindling for an outdoor fire before going off to fish. Her mother would not be with her today. She planned to help a woman who had slipped and hurt herself. Inerluk worked at finishing the herring net, because he had had enough exercise for today.

From where Nedercook fished today she could see quite a distance up the side of one of the hills. As she fished, she recalled that her mother used to tell her about the grave that stood alone on the high hillside. She remembered her mother saying:

> Some years ago, as was the case in Alaska long ago, the early days of spring always brought a certain amount of hard times. These were the days when the

food that had been put up for winter was usually gone. There would not be much food around for a time but a few tomcod.

One man in the village of Rocky Point was a very good hunter. He had been out hunting and came back with a black whale. He knew that his sister, who lived on another part of the point, was also hard up for food. He sent a man to go and bring his sister over to feast.

His sister had caught a few tomcod and she was eating them when she saw the man coming. Fearing that something had befallen her brother, she accidently swallowed a large fish bone. She started out with the man, going to the village, but she made it only half way. The bone made her throat swell so it closed shut and choked her. She was buried there high on the hill where she had died.

As she continued to fish her mind turned to Oopick. She too was now in a grave, and Nedercook remembered how Oopick used to tell her of things long, long past. One tale began:

Long, long ago, when the village was small and the people decided that they wanted to have a village here, the elders voiced their disapproval of anyone running away from the village. They said that others who had run away from their village became what was called Ie-thre-gook (one who hides from other people). They have skin that has dried to their bones. They cannot die, but whistle through their dried lips, and when they are thirsty and want a drink, the water recedes.

Nedercook remembered how Oopick would not say, "This is untrue," but made Nedercook understand that it was just an old story of long, long ago. As she fished, Nedercook wondered whether anyone ever had run away from her village and dried up. She dismissed it and remembered something else she had heard. On the other side of Rocky Point, inland and back from where the Women of the Sea fished, but near enough that it is called Cheer-kook, is a large lake. It is supposed to be inhabited by a strange animal. If people swim in it, they are always drowned, they are always pulled to the bottom. This made her feel spooky just thinking about it, especially as the day was getting on, so she loaded up the sled and returned home. She had fished enough for today.

That evening her father said, "You have learned nearly all the stories. There are two or three left," and he began:

Once there were a man and a woman who were living as man and wife. The man went out seal hunting and came home dragging a seal. She ran down joyously to meet him and help drag it back. He would not let her help him with it. She offered to help cut it up.

"No," he said, "I am going to do it myself."

So she offered to cook it.

"No," he said, "I am going to cook it and feed myself." When it was time to eat, he would not let her eat any because he was going to feed himself. Hurt and discouraged, she left him and moved to another part of the village. All that summer she gathered berries and put them up for the coming winter. When winter came, hunters traded other foods for her berries. Later a famine struck the village and everyone was hungry except the woman who had picked all the berries.

One day her husband came to her place while she was eating berries mixed with Eskimo ice cream. He said, "I want some of your berries."

She remembered the times she had begged, and he had not given her even a mouthful of food. So she said, "No, I am going to feed myself," and she kept on eating.

He was thin and he repeated, "Let me have some berries."

"No, I am going to feed myself," she answered, but he persisted.

She then sucked a seed of the salmonberry and she threw the seed out onto the dirt floor in front of him, repeating, "I'll feed myself." He scrambled to find it in the dim light, and as he searched for it he collapsed and died.

172

CHAPTER 25
ROCKS

After the cold, dark nights of winter these nice days seemed to pass quickly for Nedercook. Now it was time for her brothers to get ready to go on the black whale hunt, the most exciting of all hunts.

All the men who were going on this hunt would gather the night before, in a cave, and sing and go through motions of spearing the whale, preparing for the hunt. This practice was to insure success.

The first evening Nedercook worried a little about her brothers. As her parents settled for the night, her father said, "Tell one more story," and so he began:

> Long ago they say that in this village there was a brother and sister. They lived in different parts of this big village of Rocky Point. The sister had put up a seal poke of half-dried salmon which they called Un-I-Mark.
>
> One day the brother sent a young man to his sister's for some of the half-dried fish. He said, "Your brother sent me for some of your half-dried fish."
>
> "No," she replied, "When the sun reaches that bump on the horizon there will be a storm."
>
> Her brother's feelings were very badly hurt. All of the people of the village were gathered at the Big Dance House and heard that his sister had refused to send him any fish. (People attending usually brought some food.)
>
> When spring came, the brother went hunting and got a black whale. He brought it to shore and the job of cutting it up began. While he was doing this, his sister came carrying the seal poke of half-dried fish and said to her brother and his helpers. "Here, help yourselves to this."

173

Her brother told his sister to take her bag of fish back home, as he said, "When the sun reaches that bump on the horizon there will be another storm, you can eat it then." He also told his helpers not to give her any of the whale. This time it was her feelings that were hurt. She returned home carrying her seal poke. After she had eaten up all the half-dried fish, she was found dead, starved to death.

Next morning Inerluk said to Nedercook, "Today we go see rocks." He put some food into his packsack as he continued, "I have taken all my children on this walk when they were old enough to remember. Now it is time for you to know the rocks."

Nedercook removed her soft-soled, slipper-like boots which she wore around the inne. Taking a handful of dry grass, she broke it by folding several inches over. Then from the broken end of the grass she roughly measured the length of the sole of her mukluk. Then she bent and folded the other end of the grass over to the same size and inserted it into the mukluk with the folded ends underneath. This would serve as the inner sole. She fixed the other the same way. Then she put on these walking mukluks which had harder soles of oogruk. She put some dry fish into her pack and she was ready.

Today Inerluk said they would go toward Little Rocky Point. They called the long end of land that protruded into the sea Big Rocky Point, and the smaller one Little Rocky Point.

Nedercook was always happy when walking the tundra, rocks and beaches. Some of the birds were nesting now, so they were not singing as much as they did earlier in the spring, but robins, sparrows and other little tundra birds sang.

Father and daughter walked from the old winter camp, passed the rocks from which Nedercook often fished, and walked on until they came to the stone that looked like a man sitting down. Inerluk told his daughter what he had been told about this man-like rock. Then they walked on until they came to where there was an indentation in the rocks that looked just as if two caribou had bedded down. In between there was a big scratch mark.

Inerluk, walking ahead, heard Nedercook say in a hushed tone, "Papa." He turned to see his daughter pointing ahead. He smiled at her. "It is like the man rock. This one is walrus." Nedercook walked close to her father until she was sure the walrus-like form was really made of stone. Then she walked ahead, her dark eyes bright with excitement. Inerluk answered her questions as best he could.

"Now we go there and eat," Inerluk said as he raised a hand and pointed to a little knoll off in the distance. The walk over the tundra was easy and shortly after noon they reached the knoll. From the sea a warm spring breeze blew.

Inerluk removed his pack and sat down. Nedercook did the same, but sat so she could see behind her father. This was a precautionary measure the villagers took so they could eat in peace, with no worry of something sneaking up behind. When they finished eating, Inerluk said, "See that." Nedercook looked at a big, dry hole which had an oblong shape. Then she saw the marks that showed in front, leading away toward the salty waters of Golovin Bay. As her father sat on the knoll he looked down toward the big grass-covered hole. "When I was young," he said, "there was a little water still in it. At that time one could see clearly the markings going from it. The people said that, before my time, this was a lake, and a very large animal (his description sounded like a dinosaur) was living in this lake. When the water started to recede, the large animal decided to go to the sea water of Golovin Bay. He burned the land as he went, leaving a trail like someone had rolled down

175

across the tundra. When the animal reached the salt water he is supposed to have died in it. The lake he had lived in dried up after he left. Now it is just a big depression grown over with grass."

"See that place down there," her father said as he pointed toward the shoreline. Nedercook looked. "That," he said, "was where your grandmother used to have her fish cache."

After they got to their feet her father pointed toward Big Rocky Point. "Too far today, but soon we go there. I show you big cave where men go to perform rituals before going on big black whale hunt in the spring. We will make a trip to the top of the highest hill (elevation 1,688 feet). There you will see a very, very old ring of driftwood that makes a complete circle around this, the highest hill. In the center at the top it looks like someone during the big flood had tried to make a shelter. When we return from that trip we will come back by the cliffs there. I will show you where there is a mark on the cliff. It is like a big king salmon has slapped his tail against the cliff. We will come back above the big crack that runs up the cliff. I will show you the little trail, which we must not take. If a dog takes this trail it always falls to its death. The trip will be a long one for you, but you should see these things so you, too, will know."

CHAPTER 26
SPRING

As Nedercook and her parents sat around the dying embers of the dinner fire, Kiachook sat as if she was unaware of her husband's eyes, as they kept scanning the waters for their sons' return. She knew her husband was thinking of Nutchuk and Oolark, out at sea. This was the first year he had not gone on the black whale hunt, but he had let his sons take his oomiak as captains, with a crew of their choice, which included Kimik.

Kiachook would do what she could to make the wait for their sons' return pass easier for her husband. She would make this outdoor part last as long as there was light enough for him to see any object on the distant waters. Turning her head toward her daughter, she said, "I sing short old song." She began with humming:

The Man From Rocky Point
Long ago there was a man
living at Rocky Point.
He walked to the rocks,
Whales and seals were swimming
toward the shore.
They were feeding on the schools of fish
that were there. He stood looking
and wishing that he had a spear.
All that he had was a bob-tailed weasel skin,
which was his charm or idol
or good luck piece.

Then, as unexpected by her husband as it was by Nedercook, her mother began a story:

177

One spring some years ago, when starvation was spreading through the village, one man left in a blizzard to go and try fishing for tomcod. He met a caribou, who changed into a man. "A wolf is after me and I need help. Save me from the wolf and I will pay you back. Hide me quick." And he changed back into a caribou.

Grabbing the caribou, the fisherman sang and patted it. As he did so the animal became smaller and smaller until he could put it into his hunting sack. He met the wolf and the wolf asked him if he had seen any caribou. "No," he said, as he had the caribou in his hunting sack.

After the wolf left he took the caribou from the sack and the caribou told him, "When you get to your camp, go out a little ways from your camp and jump the best way you can." People of his village were starving and weak, but the next morning when he got up he went a little ways from camp and he jumped as best he could. He landed on top of a big black whale. He went back to get the people and they all came with him. There was no more starvation.

When Kiachook finished the story a faraway look came into her eyes, as she looked across the calm waters. As if deciding on something, she moved a little closer to the fire and added some small twigs that threw a cheerful light about them. "Daughter," Kiachook said, "In years past when I was confronted with a very puzzling question, one beyond any answer that I could find but one that needed an answer, there was one way I found an answer.

"I would bind the feet and arms of a person. Then using a piece of wood, I would put it under the person's calf and try to lift. Then I would place it under the base of the neck and try. 'Yes' was the answer when no power I used could raise either end. 'No' was when little effort raised either end of a person.

"I used to do this in the earlier days, before you were born," Kiachook continued. "Back in those days there were many puzzling questions, that seemed to have no answers until I asked, but things are changing now. I have seen it. There will be more changes too where our people are concerned. Somehow I feel it, daughter, in a strange way that I cannot put into words. But you are young, note the way we live now, like I did in my youth, and watch as the years pass — you will see."

"Car-car." Suddenly a raven interrupted her. Looking at it winging by, Kiachook said, "They say that the raven is a wise bird," she continued as if talking to herself. "Perhaps the raven thinks I talk too much. Maybe I do, but I think I should tell you about the Oook-ka-mute. These people lived in the direction the sun rises in midsummer. They lived near the mouth of the large river. We had heard many things about how differently these people lived from us, how they did not keep their bodies clean.

"Once long ago, two of these men came to our village. They both wore caps that fit close over the tops of their heads. The caps were made of sealskin with the skin side next to the head. We were short of food and had opened a hole of the food we called rotten (salmon heads), and when they came in and smelled it they acted like they wanted some. When it was offered to them, they removed their round, bowl-like caps and put the food in them. Looking inside of the caps one knew they used them for their eating dishes. When they had finished eating they put their hats back on."

Kiachook paused as if remembering that long ago day. The light on the water was dim by now and the coals nearly gone. "Tomorrow we walk up to high place and look," Kiachook said. Nedercook felt happy. She loved walking on the tundra and hills. Now it had the good smells of spring, the little tundra birds would sing, and new plants would be starting to grow.

Dusk had fallen; it was time to enter the inne. As Nedercook rose her mind was on thoughts of the coming day, and she did not see until too late that her mukluk toe had turned over the bowl of seal oil, spilling it to

179

be lost in the cracks of the earth below her.

"Mama!" she cried in panic as she realized what she had done.

Kiachook valued food as much as anyone, but she knew the oil was beyond recovery. So she said what she had been taught to say whenever food was accidently lost. "That will be for grandpa," Kiachook said as she picked up the empty bowl and carried it into the inne.

When they had settled for the night, Nedercook's father spoke, saying, "Tell you last new story." He began:

> This story is one that has been handed down from years and years ago. It is about King Island.
>
> King Island was supposed to be originally an inland mountain, and years ago it was supposed to be connected by a channel of water to the sea.
>
> The start of King Island was when a big piece of land broke loose from a mountain and went seaward, diving up and down, like a big whale, but when it reached its present location and was surfacing, a raven flying by speared it. It turned into the present island and moved no more. In ancient times the top seemed to have a large spear protruding from it.
>
> Later an old grandmother and granddaughter inhabited the island. When greens would appear in the spring they would always go out to pick them. On one trip they found some very young cormorants and carried them back home.
>
> One day after berry-picking they returned to find that someone must have been in their house while they were away, as everything was all mixed up. After a time they became suspicious because it looked like the doings of people. One day after preparing to go out to pick berries or greens, they hid out near the door. They heard the sound of human voices inside and they entered suddenly. There were the young cormorants as human beings. Surprising them broke the spell. They could not return to their cormorant forms, so they remained as human beings.
>
> Thus began the people of the island and their accent,

181

which the Rocky Point people always referred to as similar to that of a cormorant's noise.

The first generation was supposed to bear the flat head of the cormorant. Later generations had normally shaped heads.

When Inerluk finished he said, "This story was of long, long ago. Things have changed since then and the people of King Island no longer remind anyone of cormorants."

Next morning dawned calm, clear and warm. Nedercook ran to the little knoll above their inne, as she often did, and looked across the water. Far off she could see a dark object. She turned her head away and then looked again; it was still there. Back to the inne she ran. As she was about to enter, her parents came out. "See something dark on water," she said excitedly. All hurried to the little knoll.

Inerluk stood with one hand shading his eyes, then his face broke into a big smile. "Our relatives come," he said with happiness and relief. Nedercook hopped about on the knoll and said as if to herself, "They are coming, they are coming."

Great excitement stirred the villagers as they watched the approaching oomiak. As it drew nearer they could see that it was towing a darker object. The villagers were happy. Around the fires on the beach tonight there would be much feasting.

Nedercook felt that she could hardly wait for the oomiak's arrival, it moved so slowly over the water. She went to the knoll. As she stood tall on the little knoll, she saw her parents and people of the village going to the beach. She knew they were going to start the fires and put the pots of water to heat.

Just then a swallow flew past her. With the arrival of the swallows her people believed that the freezing nights were over. Happiness flowed through her parka-clad body as she breathed in the sweet air and whispered, "Spring," than ran toward the beach.

About the Author

Edna Wilder was born in Bluff, Alaska, at that time a small mining community just northwest of Rocky Point, where this story takes place. She is the daughter of the late Minnie Nedercook and Arthur Samuel Tucker.

Sam Tucker came over from England to cross Chilkoot Pass. On the other side of the pass were the Klondyke and the 1898 gold rush. Soon afterward, gold was found on the beaches of Nome. Tucker floated down the Yukon River on a raft, going to Nome. At this time Minnie Nedercook was a young woman in the village of Rocky Point. Edna wrote about their life together in her book *The Eskimo Girl and the Englishman*, published in 2008 by the University of Alaska Press.

Edna was one of Sam and Minnie Tucker's five children and grew up in Bluff. She married the late Dan C. Wilder and moved from Nome to Fairbanks, where her creative career began. She paints in watercolor and oil, and sculpts with wood and soapstone. She has instructed classes in skin-sewing and basket-weaving at the University of Alaska Fairbanks. Her art appeared in the A-67 Centennial Exposition in Fairbanks in 1967 and a Fairbanks Art Association show in 1969. In 1980 her paintings and sculptures were shown at the Charles and Emma Frye Museum in Seattle.

Her first book, *Secrets of Eskimo Skin Sewing*, is available from the University of Alaska Press.

Now Mrs. Alexander P. Cryan, Edna lives and works in Fairbanks.